WIL...

New Castle Co Del.
Scale 45 rods to the inch.

Wauzeka Oil Co
S. E. Thompson & Co

Shell Pot Cr.

R I V E R

4TH WARD

R I V E R

Coal Yard of
N.W. Taylor & Th...

Burton McCaulley & Co
Ship & Steam Boat Works
Marine Rail Way

Ship Yard
Marine R. Way

E & C. Moore

Car Shops P.W. & B.R.R.
Shops

Swedes Ch.
Cem.

Boiler St.

Wilmington Rolling Mill Co

2ND WARD

Christiana Light House

CHRISTIANA

AVENUE

HEALD ST.
CLAYMONT ST.
CHURCH

DUNCAN

ST.
ST.
ST.
ST.

AVE. AVE. AVE. AVE. AVE. AVE. AVE.

8TH 8TH 4TH 3D 2D 1ST

Wilmington, Delaware

Portrait of an Industrial City

1830–1910

Wilmington, Delaware
Portrait of an Industrial City

1830–1910 , 1974 .

Carol E. Hoffecker

Published for the Eleutherian Mills–Hagley Foundation
by the University Press of Virginia

THE UNIVERSITY PRESS OF VIRGINIA

Copyright © 1974 by the Eleutherian Mills–Hagley Foundation

First published 1974

ISBN: 0–8139–0519–2
Library of Congress Catalog Card Number: 73–88917
Printed in the United States of America

Birds Eye View of the City of Wilmington, Del. Drawn ca. 1865 by E. Sachse & Co. of Baltimore. The view is from south to north, with the Christina River at the bottom and the Brandywine toward the top. Note the path of the P.W.&B.R.R. (Courtesy H.S.D.)

To my parents
Ralph Charles Hoffecker
and
Kathryn Zebley Hoffecker
both born and reared in Wilmington

Contents

Preface

Today when the future of urban life is so uncertain there is a particular need for Americans to retrace the process by which the United States became an urban nation. The study of the dynamic elements that have shaped urban growth will help to inform present-day discussion of how to reinvigorate American cities. Evidence concerning the history of cities survives in two forms: written materials, including newspapers, annual reports, and the like, and physical remains, including houses, factories, streets, and utilities. The latter confront us every day and are frequently considered part of the current problem of decay. The former, while less noticeable, are a necessary aid toward the understanding of the physical remains, explaining how they came to be and what they represented to the generations that produced them.

I began this enquiry into Wilmington's past by taking walks through various neighborhoods of the city. Like many other American communities, Wilmington today can be described as a collection of modern high-rise office buildings surrounded by older houses and parking lots. In a few places urban renewal has replaced the nineteenth-century row houses with fake-colonial modern ones or has left large stretches of land vacant. The city is ringed by extensive white suburbs that have a much larger population than the city proper in which blacks predominate in many areas.

In crucial ways the Wilmington of the 1970s is entirely different from its predecessor in the era before the automobile, the suburb, the shopping mall, and the large science-oriented corporations that have made their homes here. Despite these differences, however, we have much to learn from the past. Not only its physical remains but its community spirit, its hopes and fears, its failures and successes can tell us something about both the causes and cures of our current problems. In this belief I have undertaken to write an account of Wilmington in the middle years of its development, the years roughly from 1830 to 1910, when the city grew from its colonial origins as a milling and shipping town into an industrial center.

My thanks are due to many people and institutions who have aided me in this study but most especially to Walter J. Heacock, General Director of

Preface   the Eleutherian Mills–Hagley Foundation, and Richmond D. Williams, Director of the Eleutherian Mills Historical Library, who offered me a fellowship and then a succession of posts at the Eleutherian Mills Historical Library and the Hagley Museum while I worked on the project. Without their support I could certainly never have written this book. The Eleutherian Mills Historical Library staff has been extremely helpful throughout my study. To Mrs. Betty-Bright Low and Mrs. Carol Hallman of the Research and Reference Department together with Miss Julia F. Davis and her successor Mr. Daniel Muir and Miss Marjorie Gregory of the Pictorial Collections Department I owe a particular debt. The staffs of Special Collections at the Morris Library, University of Delaware, the Delaware State Archives, and the Wilmington Institute Free Library have also been unfailingly helpful, as were Mrs. Gladys M. Coghlan and Miss Joanne Mattern of the Historical Society of Delaware.

    A number of persons assisted me in the preparation of the manuscript. David T. Gilchrist, Director of Publications, Eleutherian Mills–Hagley Foundation, and Richard Ehrlich, Assistant to the Director of the Eleutherian Mills Historical Library, read the manuscript and made many helpful suggestions toward its improvement. My parents aided in the identification of some of the pictures, and Miss Joann Silverberg read the manuscript in several stages and offered suggestions regarding its style and content. Last but hardly least, I must thank Mrs. Ella Phillips, who interrupted her numerous duties to type the manuscript.

Introduction

Historians of urban America have often argued that community spirit and social cohesion gradually declined as American cities industrialized in the nineteenth century. Centering on the difficulties faced by immigrants and on public apathy toward political corruption, historians have declared that, in spite of the glitter that lured many into urban life, Americans came to regard their cities as desperately lonely, unforgiving places as epitomized by Theodore Dreiser's pictures of Chicago and New York life in *Sister Carrie.* The most recent exposition of this thesis of communal disintegration is Sam Bass Warner's *The Private City,* a study of the process of urbanization during three distinct periods in Philadelphia's development. Concentrating his study on five aspects of urban life—population growth, the course of industrialization, the changing locations of places of work and homes, the shifting intensity of residential clusters, and the group organization of work—Warner concluded that the spirit of "privatism" was the key to the atrophy of social integration. According to his model, social harmony characterized the colonial and federal periods when Philadelphia was a "walking city" composed largely of household shops integrated into neighborhoods, each of which included a cross section of the total social fabric. This fabric was shattered in the course of the nineteenth century by forces such as immigration and ethnic heterogeneity, industrialization, and the business leaders' loss of interest in local problems. The "Big City" of the 1860s had become the mecca of private money-makers whose indifference to communal concerns rendered Philadelphia unhealthy, unfriendly, and unsafe. "The mass of city dwellers," he found, "lacked any effective means to humanize their lives," while "the rich, using their wealth to create insulated enclaves within the city or beyond it, escaped the constraints of commonplace urban life."[1] In such a setting community life was impossible, and the stage was set for the urban failures of our own time.

[1] Sam B. Warner, *The Private City: Philadelphia in Three Periods of Its Growth* (Philadelphia, 1968), p. ix.

Introduction This book presents a corrective for, though not a replacement of, the view that urban communality was prevented by excessive individualism. It argues that in some ways community spirit and social institutions were strengthened as the processes of urbanization unfolded to create wholly new social forms. The remarkable developments in transportation and manufacturing initiated during the first half of the century drew large numbers of people into urban areas, altered the class structure of cities, and undermined social forms inherited from the past. City dwellers confronted unprecedented problems in the readjustment of both their private lives and civic structures. It was only because of the zest that urbanites displayed for creating a host of new social institutions that humane urban life was possible in the industrial age. The dynamics of their response was impressively wide-ranging and inclusive.

When Alexis de Tocqueville visited the United States during the 1830s he was amazed at the number and influence of nonpolitical as well as political associations among the Americans. "The political associations that exist in the United States," he wrote, "are only a single feature in the midst of the immense assemblage of associations in that country. Americans of all ages, all conditions, and all dispositions constantly form associations. They have not only commercial and manufacturing companies, in which all take part, but associations of a thousand other kinds, religious, moral, serious, futile, general or restricted, enormous or diminutive."[2] At that time civic-minded persons organized a variety of new institutions, such as public schools, asylums, and literary societies, designed to bring stability and moral order to American life, especially in urban centers.[3] Religious institutions, traditionally the mainstays of orderly community life, likewise engaged in an expanded effort to maintain order and provide useful services in towns and cities. Institution-building was a cumulative phenomenon in the development of American urban society, and as the century progressed city dwellers created more civic groups and dramatically increased public services. Philanthropies were more rationally organized in the associated charities movement of the 1860s and 1870s in an effort to systematize private welfare. Meanwhile the press of humanity into the cities generated the

---

[2] Alexis de Tocqueville, *Democracy in America*, 2 vols. (New York, 1945), 2:106.

[3] David J. Rothman, *Discovery of the Asylum: Social Order and Disorder in the New Republic* (Boston, 1971); and Robert Wiebe, *The Search for Order* (New York, 1968).

xii

need for various civic improvements in water supply, sanitation, transportation, and safety. The satisfaction of these needs depended upon the expansion of the function of municipal government as well as technological innovations. In addition, volunteer fire companies, athletic, cultural, and ethnic associations as well as fraternal orders blossomed as people turned to social activities outside the home to occupy their leisure time and to fulfill various health, business, and welfare needs. The result was the modern city, a complex organism encompassing many interacting public and private organizations.

The first step toward a fuller understanding of the dynamics of communal life in nineteenth-century cities is to recognize that each city had unique qualities. Numerous factors determined a city's pattern of development and the vitality and influence of both its public and private organizations and institutions. Size, rate of growth, and economic conditions were the most significant factors in the framework of a city's social system. For example, a city that had large numbers of unskilled workers and absentee ownership of its industries was less likely to develop strong community institutions than a city that had a well-established middle class. Stephen Thernstrom showed in his statistical study of upward mobility among unskilled laborers in mid-nineteenth-century Newburyport, Massachusetts, *Poverty and Progress*,[4] that most of his subjects led peripatetic lives. Like many modern Americans, these workers often did not stay in any one place long enough to develop communal ties. The relative size of various social classes within a community was a function of that city's economy. An unusually high incidence of unskilled and semiskilled workers proportional to skilled and white-collar workers militated against strong social organization. Vera Shlakman pointed out in her study of Chicopee, Massachusetts, *The Economic History of a Factory Town*, that a community composed of poorly paid imported mill hands offered few opportunities for middle-class retailers and professionals who might have formed the backbone of a fuller community life.[5]

Wilmington, Delaware, the city that I have chosen to demonstrate nineteenth-century community development, was unusually well-rounded in

[4] Stephen Thernstrom, *Poverty and Progress* (Cambridge, Mass., 1964).
[5] Vera Shlakman, *Economic History of a Factory Town: A Study of Chicopee, Massachusetts* (New York, 1969).

terms of its class structure, ethnic composition, and economy. A small industrial city that in the nineteenth century never exceeded a hundred thousand persons, it was located twenty-seven miles south of Philadelphia on the Delaware River. The only city in the otherwise rural state of Delaware, Wilmington was both a satellite of the Pennsylvania metropolis and a minor commercial and industrial center in its own right. Nineteenth-century Wilmington was ethnically diverse. As the century opened, English Quakers and Scotch-Irish were the most prominent groups in the town's population, but with Wilmington's early advent into the industrial age many Irish and Germans settled there. By 1860 the foreign born accounted for 18.86 percent of Wilmington's population; after that their importance declined somewhat to 13.6 percent in 1900.[6] The black community comprised approximately 10 percent of the city's population throughout the nineteenth century.

Wilmington's history can be conveniently divided into three distinct periods, based on shifts in its major economic functions. Beginning as a grain-processing and -distributing center with close ties to Philadelphia, Wilmington adopted a predominantly industrial economy in the 1840s when new methods of transportation were undermining its commercial enterprises. Shipbuilding, railroad-car construction, carriage making, and iron founding—industries that were for the most part owned and managed by local men and that demanded a high percentage of skilled workers—flourished in the years between 1840 and 1900. Although Wilmington had a port engaging in some ocean and much river commerce, the city was primarily industrial in that period. In the early twentieth century most of these industries began to decline, and the community structure, which had accompanied industrialization characterized by large numbers of blue-collar workers and an elite of factory owners, lost importance in the community. As heavy industry faded, Wilmington developed yet another economic function—that of management and research, the result of the Du Pont Company's decision to locate its major offices in the city.

Wilmington entered the industrial age with few social institutions and a weak municipal government featuring a nearly powerless executive branch, continual state intervention in local affairs, and similar weaknesses common

[6] U.S. Census 1860, *Population* (Washington, D.C., 1866), 1: xxxii; 1910, *Population* (Washington, D.C., 1913), 2:282.

to most city charters of the time. A city not noted for social innovation, Wilmington's leaders and journalists constantly despaired of the apathy of their town. Yet, despite these limitations, in the years that followed, especially during the two decades after the Civil War, its citizens created numerous new public and private organizations and greatly extended the influence of those already in existence. Charitable institutions and fraternal orders proliferated, public and parochial school systems were developed, churches sprang up everywhere, and new opportunities for amusement and for athletics became available to all classes. The city government became much more responsive to public demands for services. Water supplies were enlarged, streets and sewers built, and several parks were established. Meanwhile, trolley companies knit the growing city together and provided amusement parks on its outskirts. All of these developments made for new patterns of social cohesion and offered most citizens expanded opportunities for communal life unmatched by those of the preindustrial past.

The most striking causal factor throughout this period of development was the important role played by the upper middle class, professional men, industrial entrepreneurs, and their families, in bringing the new Wilmington into being. If the city's wealthy men had been absentee factory owners, or even if they had chosen to build their residence outside the city in some detached suburb, it is doubtful that many of the public improvements outlined in this book would have come to pass. It was the business leaders' commitment to their city more than any other single factor that made industrial Wilmington a livable city for most of its residents. This commitment was prompted by economic necessity as much as by civic pride, for the industrial leaders of this small city recognized that their business success depended on the image of progress and modernity Wilmington projected. Even though Wilmington had numerous tanneries, foundries, shipbuilding firms and the like, the men who owned these businesses saw themselves in competition with rivals in other cities rather than with one another. Wilmington's industrialists and retailers had a great stake in making certain that their community was sufficiently well governed and attractive to draw customers, workers, and new industry to their city.

Abbreviations

A.S.D.	Archives of the State of Delaware
E.M.H.L.	Eleutherian Mills Historical Library
H.M.M.L.	Hugh M. Morris Library, University of Delaware
H.S.D.	Historical Society of Delaware
W.I.F.L.	Wilmington Institute Free Library

Note: Uncredited illustrations are from the author's collection.

Wilmington, Delaware

Portrait of an Industrial City

1830–1910

1. *View of Wilmington, Del.* View from the Southwest, "Drawn From Nature and on Stone by E. Whitefield in the Year 1851." The Newport Turnpike, now Maryland Avenue, can be seen to the left, the Christina River and the P.W.&B.R.R. to the right. (Courtesy E.M.H.L.)

CHAPTER I

The Process of Industrialization

The Town and Its Economy

Early in 1638 two small ships, the *Kalmar Nyckel* and *Vogel Grip*, bearing an advance guard of soldiers, traders, and artisans, arrived in the Delaware River to found the colony of New Sweden. As they sailed up the Delaware, the colonists saw flat marshlands along the west bank penetrated by a series of small rivers. Continuing up stream they arrived at a place where a placid river flowed into the Delaware. Upon entering this little river, they very quickly came to a fork. The southern branch, navigable for more than a mile inland, meandered through low-lying fields. The character of the northerly branch was quite different: less than one mile upstream it gave way to rushing white water falling rapidly from the hilly, heavily forested country to the northwest. Between these streams overlooking the Delaware River marshes was a gently sloping hill. Here, alongside the southerly navigable stream, the colonists had been instructed to build a settlement, which they named Fort Christina in honor of their youthful queen. The settlers named the navigable waterway on which their colony fronted the Christina River (known as the Christiana River during the nineteenth century). Its rocky companion came to be called the Brandywine.

The history of New Sweden proved to be a short one. With much land in the home country as yet unsettled, Sweden was not prepared to support the mass migrations to America that might have brought success in the highly competitive enterprise of imperial adventuring. Within twenty-six years of its founding, New Sweden was successively captured, first by the Dutch, then by the English. The Dutch eschewed Fort Christina in favor of a settlement called New Amstel, which they established directly on the Delaware River about six miles to the south. This town, renamed New Castle by its English conqueror, James, Duke of York, was ceded in 1682 to William Penn, who made it the county seat of New Castle County, the most northerly of his "three lower counties."

By the 1730s the Fort Christina settlement had nearly ceased to exist. A few descendants of the Swedish colonists remained near their stone Lutheran church, built on the banks of the Christina in 1698, but the remnants of settlement between the Christina and Brandywine had scant economic or political significance. Residents of the town of New Castle traded directly with Europe or Philadelphia via the Delaware River, ignoring the old Swedish settlement. Then in the 1730s increased population in the interior regions of Pennsylvania gave impetus to renewed urbanization at the confluence of the three rivers. The establishment of Lancaster, Pennsylvania, in 1730 signaled the westward movement of the farming frontier. From many parts of Lancaster and Chester counties, the shortest route for grain to the Delaware River and thence to Philadelphia was by wagon to the Christina, which was navigable for small riverboats from the modern town of Newport just west of Wilmington, eastward to the Delaware.[1]

Probably in response to the opportunities made possible by this emerging trade pattern, a group of Quaker families from Ridley, Pennsylvania, south of Philadelphia on the Delaware River, migrated to the banks of the Christina. Two Englishmen were chiefly responsible for reconstituting the town, Thomas Willing and William Shipley. Willing inherited land along the Christina River adjacent to the Swedish hamlet. Concluding that the area could become a shipping center for grain, he laid out lots in 1731 on a grid pattern copied directly from Penn's Philadelphia. Until 1735 when William Shipley moved from Ridley to the new town, however, Willingtown was just a plan on paper. Shipley's wife, a prominent religious leader among the Friends, made frequent trips to attend Quaker meetings throughout the region. According to legend she dreamt that her family would settle in a valley near two rivers, one swift and rocky, the other calm and navigable. Upon seeing the site of Willingtown during a journey, she recognized it as the land of her dream and persuaded her husband and some of her neighbors in Ridley to move to the new town.[2] The Shipleys and the other families of Friends who came bought land from Willing and undertook the creation of a commercial center along the Christina. The newcomers erected brick homes and quickly turned Willingtown into a local farmers' market and a point of transshipment for grain brought from the farms of Lancaster, Chester, and New Castle counties en route to Philadelphia. Shipley also took the lead in town government. He founded a market and petitioned

[1] James T. Lemon, "Urbanization and the Development of Eighteenth-Century Southeastern Pennsylvania and Adjacent Delaware," *William and Mary Quarterly* 24 (1967): 526.
[2] J. Thomas Scharf, *History of Delaware*, 2 vols. (Philadelphia, 1888), 2:632.

4

King George II for borough status for the community. The king granted this request in 1739, with the stipulation that the town's name be changed to Wilmington in honor of one of the king's friends. The borough charter created a council of seven burgesses and other annually elected officials to administer the markets and keep the peace.[3]

The town grew steadily. In 1739, 610 persons lived in Wilmington. The Quaker families, Canby and Tatnall, built gristmills along the nearby Brandywine where they established a tiny satellite community called

[3] *Ibid.,* 2:636.

2. *Brandywine Grist Mills at Market Street Bridge.* Photograph, ca. 1865, looking northwest. (Courtesy E.M.H.L.)

Wilmington,
Delaware

Brandywine Village. By the 1770s the population had increased to about 1,230,[4] and the mills were sending as many as thirty thousand barrels of flour to Philadelphia each year and were probably capable of exporting an equal amount directly from Wilmington to the West Indies or Ireland.[5] Local

[4] *Ibid.,* 2:639.
[5] Sally G. Farris, "The Wilmington Merchant, 1775–1815" (M.A. thesis, University of Delaware, 1961), p. 20.

3. *Brandywine Village in the 1890s.* Looking north on North Market Street toward the spire of St. John's P.E. Church. The stone houses in the foreground date from the colonial period. The stuccoed house was built in 1770 by Joseph Tatnall, who entertained Washington and Lafayette there. (Courtesy H.S.D.)

merchants imported Irish linens, coffee, rum, molasses, and other foreign products at Wilmington's docks on the Christina. Shipbuilding and coopering, closely linked to the milling and shipping business became important to the town's economy. During the eighteenth century new settlers from Northern Ireland were attracted to the town. These Scotch-Irish formed Wilmington's first Presbyterian congregation in 1740; by 1774 they had established a second church.

The first settlers created a community of unpaved tree-lined streets, a miniature version of colonial Philadelphia, the socially integrated "walking city" of artisan households and mercantile offices that Sam B. Warner described in *The Private City*.[6] Home construction followed the Philadelphia fashion of three- to four-story brick townhouses with rear gardens for the well-to-do and smaller wooden or brick houses, sometimes duplexes, for the less wealthy. In contrast to later eras, the well-to-do did not congregate in any one section of the town but lived near their work. Millers built large homes of Brandywine riverbed granite close to the mills. Persons in mercantile pursuits preferred to live along Front Street, which paralleled the Christina or in the nearby Quaker Hill area along West Street between Front and Fourth. The small business district centered around lower Market Street, which ran perpendicular to the river. Artisan shops were scattered throughout the community, but specialized trades tended to congregate together in areas adjacent to the industries they served. Those engaged in shipbuilding settled near Front Street, while coopers abounded in Brandywine Village near the mills. Scattered clusters of Negroes lived at the edges of the town on the least valuable lands.[7]

Although Wilmington lacked a commons or green, all residents had ready access to nonurban vistas for the country was only a short walk from the center of town. From their homes along Front Street, merchants could view the marshland that lay across the Christina River;[8] the east side of town, from the foot of the hill whose ridge runs along Market Street, consisted mainly of unoccupied lowlands. Just a few blocks west of Market Street, farmlands began in the midst of undulating hills.

---

[6] Sam B. Warner, *The Private City: Philadelphia in Three Periods of Its Growth* (Philadelphia, 1968).

[7] *Wilmington City Directory*, 1814. Modern street names have been used to avoid confusion.

[8] Elizabeth Montgomery, *Reminiscences of Wilmington* (Wilmington, Del., 1872), p. 188.

Wilmington,
Delaware

4. *The Bush Residence, French and Water Streets.* Samuel Bush founded in 1774 a river transport company which later became the George W. Bush and Sons Steam Freight Lines. The family home was described by Elizabeth Montgomery, *Reminiscences,* p. 188, as "elevated with a graceful slope to the water," with "a full view of the shipping." This nineteenth-century photograph shows how the P.W.&B.R.R. made the waterfront a less desirable neighborhood. (Courtesy H.S.D.)

The town's population increased to 5,000 by the second decade of the nineteenth century, but social change came slowly to Wilmington because the economic base of the town remained unaltered for a century. The same Quaker families who had set up the flour mills and established mercantile operations in the 1730s and 1740s continued to control these essential activities. The majority of the town's residents were engaged in crafts or merchandizing, trades conducted in small shops, often in the master's home. Trained in the traditional manner of apprentices, citizens of the town had little need to create innovative educational forms designed to aid mobility or to provide training in new skills. Recreation consisted of private pursuits such as hunting, fishing, and home entertainments that did not involve large organized groups or communitywide participation. The county fair, the only formal event that depended on local government, brought the entire community together annually.

Wilmington society was a mixture of simplicity and exclusivity in which social stratification determined eligibility for inclusion in the town's few educational and social organizations. Elizabeth Montgomery, the principal chronicler of late-eighteenth-century Wilmington, recalled that Quaker simplicity set the tone. "Originally settled by a people of plain manners and great integrity of character," she wrote, "[Wilmington] has afforded every accommodation without the larger expense, pretension, and embarrassment of some of the greater cities, in consequence of which a higher degree of sociability and confidence has attended a general intercourse among those persons who were entitled to enjoy it."[9] The town's leading citizens dominated few functions such as keeping the peace, regulating the weekly markets, and surveying the roadways—activities that did not require elaborate governmental organization.

The Quaker meeting was the most potent private institutional force in town life. The Friends School, established in 1748, the town's first permanent school, educated the children of Wilmington's manufacturing and mercantile leaders. Quakers also organized several of the town's modest philanthropies, the Female Benevolent Society, which supplied flax to indigent spinners, and the Humane Society, which proffered bounties to those brave enough to save people endangered by drowning, suffocation, or burning. Persons who suffered calamities of fortune or health beyond the potency of these societies retired to the public county almshouse located on the western edge of the town.

Wilmington's other denominations were expanding their activities in the early years of the nineteenth century to offer the town's children religious education. The idea of the Sunday school as a means of educating working children to read and learn the articles of the Christian faith was imported from England. Wilmington's first Sunday school was organized in 1812 by a few young men at Trinity Episcopal Church. By 1818 the school had three hundred children meeting at the Academy on Market Street for several

[9] *Ibid.*, p. 309.

9

hours each Sunday afternoon.[10] The Hanover Presbyterian Church began a similar school in 1814 under the auspices of its Female Harmony Society and soon the other congregations undertook similar activities. These schools represented the initial efforts of the churches to broaden their impact on community life. A Roman Catholic mission, St. Peter's, was established in Wilmington in 1816. In 1830 this church inaugurated an orphanage and primary school with the assistance of three Sisters of Charity from Emmitsburg, Maryland.

Those who dwelt in the big brick and stone townhouses found opportunities for organized social intercourse and intellectual development. Several private schools catered to this group. The Wilmington "college," really a classical high school, provided a background for young men destined for careers in business or the professions. The Hilles brothers, Eli and Samuel, Quakers from Chester County, Pennsylvania, offered a similar education to young ladies at their boarding school, while less academically inclined girls could attend Elizabeth Montgomery's sewing and drawing school.

In the early years of the nineteenth century, Wilmingtonians formed a variety of private organizations designed to promote philanthropic causes as well as the intellectual and social life of the town. An interdenominational Bible Society, founded in 1813, worked closely with similar societies in Philadelphia and New York to distribute religious tracts in the United States and abroad. The Library Company of Wilmington, organized in 1787, established a subscription library at the Town Hall. Within six years it had acquired nearly nine hundred volumes. The Delaware Abolition Society attracted many of Wilmington's most prominent citizens to its ranks when it was created in 1802. In the 1820s most of its members joined the Wilmington Union Colonization Society to support the migration of free blacks to Liberia. A Masonic Lodge was formed in Wilmington in 1806 by some of the town's leading citizens. In addition, the Harmonic Society, Wilmington's first musical organization founded in 1814, enjoyed phenomenal popularity. By 1816 it had attracted several hundred members each of whom paid fifty cents per quarter for the privilege of singing sacred music.[11] The number and variety of the town's organizations attests to the town's vigor at the height of the mercantile-milling economy.

[10] *Ibid.,* pp. 119–20.
[11] *Wilmington City Directory,* 1814; Scharf, *History of Delaware,* 2:817–36.

5. *The Hilles Double House, Northeast Corner of Tenth and King Streets.* Built in 1818 by the Hilles brothers, Samuel and Eli, one half was the Boarding School for Young Ladies, the other half living quarters for the Hilleses. Photograph, ca. 1912, before the block was demolished to make way for the joint city hall and county courthouse. (Courtesy E.M.H.L.)

6. *Ship Captain's and Miller's Houses*. Nos. 1300 and 1302 King Street, built ca. 1800, the former the home of Captain William Noble, the latter the home of Benjamin Price, a miller. Photograph, ca. 1950, by Frank Zebley, a descendent of the Price family.

For the less well-to-do in the community, there existed fewer opportunities for participation in formally constituted social institutions, although the town's three fire companies and five militia companies included artisans and shopkeepers among their numbers. The Mechanical Beneficial Society, formed in 1814, attracted many artisans, but unfortunately nothing is known of its activities. Work itself provided the education and social contacts for workers in an age of apprenticeships and small work groups. Shipbuilders halted work each day to drink the cup of grog that was part of their pay,[12] while the coopers lunched at midday at the sign of the Green Tree in Brandywine Village where they played handball.[13] Sailors and other dockside hands spent their free time in nearby grogshops. By the early nineteenth century, however, polite society was becoming intolerant of

[12] Montgomery, *Reminiscences*, p. 150.
[13] *Every Evening*, Jan. 25, 1894.

7. *Houses at Front and King Streets*. These colonial survivals photographed in the late nineteenth century exhibit the decline of the area near the Christina River as a residential neighborhood in the face of industrialization. (Courtesy W.I.F.L.)

working-class drinking habits. The shipbuilders daily rum ration was discontinued, and the state legislature abolished the annual county fair at Wilmington because of the excessive drinking and brawling that critics claimed accompanied the event.[14]

By later standards life in the early republic was crudely intolerant, even cruel. Mob violence was sometimes encouraged by the law, as when vagabonds were subjected to the humiliating ritual of being drummed out of town while small boys pelted them with rotten eggs.[15] Followers of unpopular causes were subjected to similar displays of ridicule. In the early days of Methodism a mob collected weekly during services at Asbury Church to break windows and hurl "nauseous reptiles, insects, and other filth . . . among the female part of the congregation."[16]

Race relations were strained by legal slavery in Delaware, but since many of those who could have afforded to keep slaves belonged to the Friends Society, which opposed slavery, the peculiar institution was practically unknown in Wilmington. The few hundred blacks who lived in the town worked mostly as domestics or in the least desirable jobs in the tanneries and shipyards. But in contrast to the later years of the nineteenth century, some blacks broke out of this occupational mold. A few became ship's carpenters or owned shops that served a white clientele. Segregation was strictly enforced by law, however. The almshouse had separate facilities for black and white inmates, while free blacks, both male and female, who were convicted of crimes were regularly subjected to the anachronistic punishment of a public whipping administered to the bare back, a sentence rarely meted out to white men and never to white women. Another punishment reserved for black convicts was being sold for a term of servitude.

The only organization that actively encouraged black membership was the Methodist Church. Methodist meetings were the most integrated feature of late eighteenth-century Wilmington's social life. Some early Methodist preachers were black, but segregationist views overcame even Methodist scruples when the meetings moved from the open air to a permanent

[14] Benjamin Ferris, *A History of the Original Settlements on the Delaware* (Wilmington, Del., 1846), p. 278.

[15] *Ibid.*, pp. 264–65.

[16] John D. C. Hanna, ed., *The Centennial Services of Asbury Methodist Episcopal Church* (Wilmington, Del., 1889), pp. 144–45.

14

building. The whites accused their black fellow members of breaking benches and tracking dirt into the church, and relegated them to the church gallery. The incensed blacks, who had experienced a degree of equality in the earlier integrated association, withdrew to found their own church in 1805.[17]

Continuity rather than change marked Wilmington's socioeconomic order in the preindustrial period. The home was the primary social institution not only in most economic activities but in entertainment and education as well. The other institutional forms outside the home—religious, governmental, educational, philanthropic, and recreational—were relatively less significant in people's lives than in the postindustrial era. Order was maintained through a system of social deference. Social roles and life-styles were carefully stratified, and the law often punished misdemeanors by methods designed to shame and humiliate. Mobility within the socioeconomic order was limited by the rigidity of the economy itself. The social institutions relevant to such a society were those that acted to perpetuate the past by preparing the younger generation to fit into the same socioeconomic roles their elders had filled.

Industrialization

The traditional economic pattern was shattered by developments in transportation and manufacturing during the years from 1840 to the Civil War. Improvements in transportation signaled the movement toward industrialization in Wilmington. Impetus for canals and railroads in the Delaware River Valley came primarily from Philadelphia, the region's premier city, which was contesting the control of markets in developing western hinterlands with New York and Baltimore. Wilmington was more often an onlooker than a partner in Philadelphia's enterprise, although the smaller city was transformed as much as Philadelphia was by the Quaker City's initiative and capital.

The transportation revolution consolidated the position of regional centers, often at the expense of lesser cities such as Wilmington, which saw its

[17] *Ibid.*, p. 146.

15

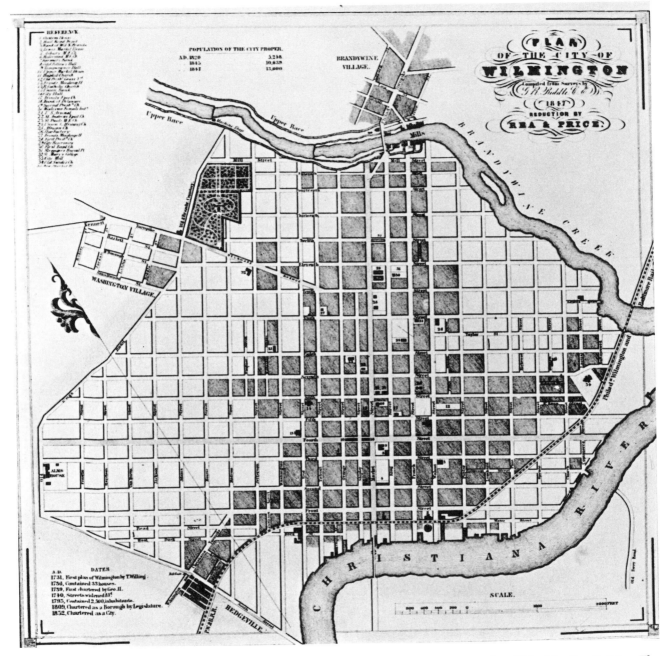

Map 1. Plan of the City of Wilmington. Surveyed by G. R. Riddle, civil engineer, in 1847 and published by Rea & Price. The earliest map of Wilmington showing the Philadelphia, Wilmington and Baltimore Railroad. The dark portions indicate the built-up parts of the city. Brandywine Village is at the top. "Washington Village" was a suburban plan that was never developed. Note also the county almshouse at the far left and the reservoir at Tenth and Market streets. (Courtesy E.M.H.L.)

hinterland being absorbed by the regional metropolis. For example, Wilmington's old economy based upon grain processing and shipping was severely curtailed by the Philadelphia-Columbia Railroad, which diverted much of the town's grain supply from southeastern Pennsylvania to Philadelphia.[18] The losses incurred in Wilmington's trade, both wholesale and retail, were more than matched, however, by new opportunities for manufactures made possible by the use of steam power on land and sea.

In 1835 a group of businessmen from Maryland, Delaware, and Pennsylvania proposed construction of a railroad to run south from Philadelphia, through Wilmington to Baltimore. Completed in 1837, the Philadelphia, Wilmington & Baltimore Railroad paralleled the Delaware River from Philadelphia to a point just north of Wilmington, then veered westward along the Christina as it passed through the Delaware town toward Maryland. The route chosen for the PW&B, located so close to the navigable Christina River, maximized the railroad's impact on Wilmington's economy because it created a prime industrial site in the narrow strip of land between the tracks and the river.

Wilmington had many advantages necessary to succeed as an independent manufacturing city in the developing industrial economy. The region around Wilmington was already one of the most important sites for water-powered industries in the United States. Mills producing paper, textiles, black powder, snuff, and flour dotted the Brandywine sharing the power generated by that rapid-falling rocky stream, while other mill sites existed on Red Clay Creek and White Clay Creek, tributaries of the Christina. Foundrymen, millwrights, and machinists as well as many other kinds of workmen whose skills were essential to the expansion of industrial technology worked in the area. These same mills also generated the capital reserves that not only made possible industrialization of the town's economy but also kept control in local hands. Furthermore, Wilmington was close to the sources of the coal and iron ore that were beginning to flow into Philadelphia from northern Pennsylvania via the new canals and railroads. Transportation of these bulk goods to Wilmington on river barges was very cheap and convenient since several Wilmington-based shipping firms maintained daily schedules of trips to and from Philadelphia.

[18] Carol E. Hoffecker, "Nineteenth-Century Wilmington: Satellite or Independent City?" *Delaware History* 15 (1972), pp. 1–18.

Map 2. Philadelphia, Wilmington and Baltimore
Railroad and Connections Taken from the *44th
Annual Report of the P.W.&B.R.R. Co., Year
Ending October 31, 1881* (Philadelphia, 1882).
(Courtesy E.M.H.L.)

8. *The Early Stages of Industry Along the Christina River.* Advertisement for Hollingsworth & Teas, *Wilmington City Directory,* 1845. Note the P.W.&B.R.R. tracks in the foreground. (Courtesy H.S.D.)

Because of these advantages, Wilmington was a hospitable location for a variety of industries. By the Civil War decade the little city could boast several cotton mills, a match factory, and a fertilizer plant. The most significant industries in Wilmington's economy, however, in terms of both employment and investment were ship and railroad-car construction, foundry work, tanning, and carriage making.[19] Railroad-car construction and its tertiary industries, coupled with shipbuilding, were on their way to becoming the city's most important activity as early as the 1840s. These industries located between the PW&B and the Christina on land that offered excellent transportation advantages but was also much cheaper than comparable locations in larger commercial cities like Philadelphia and New York. In-

[19] U.S. Census, 1860, *Manufactures* (Washington, D.C., 1866), pp. 53–54.

9. *Betts, Harlan & Hollingsworth's First Building on the Christina.* The machine shop was built in 1841 by Elijah Hollingsworth at a time when the company was concentrating on constructing railroad equipment. Drawing from *A Semi-Centennial Memoir of the Harlan & Hollingsworth Company* (Wilmington, 1886), opp. p. 177. (Courtesy E.M.H.L.)

dustrial entrepreneurs in Wilmington could also capitalize on the local tradition of skilled handling of iron and wood among workmen in the Wilmington area.

Wilmington adjusted to the new industrial economy and grew. In the process of economic change the size and character of the community was altered. These changes in the city's life can best be understood by looking more closely at the development of individual companies. At the end of the Civil War, the four largest industrial firms in Wilmington were Harlan & Hollingsworth, Pusey & Jones, The Lobdell Car Wheel Company, and Jackson & Sharp, all locally owned and all engaged in the manufacture of railroad equipment. The first two began operations in the 1830s and 1840s, respectively, on very little capital. They started at a time when the construc-

tion of railroad cars and steamships and the use of steam-powered industrial machinery were in an experimental stage. Success depended more
upon manufacturing skills and location than upon volume of production.
These companies were well located to supply cars to eastern railroads.
Harlan & Hollingsworth, which began on a $5,000 investment, within a dec-
ade acquired a forty-three-acre plot strategically located between the
Christina River and the PW&B tracks.[20]

Harlan & Hollingsworth and Pusey & Jones were successful because they
were always alive to new sales opportunities; they did not limit themselves
to car building alone but developed related specialties as well. Both pioneered in the construction of iron merchant ships, an enterprise for which
Wilmington proved to be an ideal location. Iron ships were so costly to
build that the higher labor and land costs prevailing in New York City and
Boston shipyards kept those cities out of the trade, whereas Wilmington,
according to the U.S. census report in 1880, offered low costs, and "the city
is practically as near to cheap coal and iron as though it were planted upon
the Schuylkill, and the same freight rates govern deliveries there from all

[20] Scharf, *History of Delaware*, 2:732–39.

10. *Perspective View of the
Plant of Harlan & Hollingsworth Co. in 1886*, showing
the company's extensive car
and shipbuilding facilities. *A
Semi-Centennial Memoir of
the Harlan & Hollingsworth
Company*, opp. p. 329.
(Courtesy E.M.H.L.)

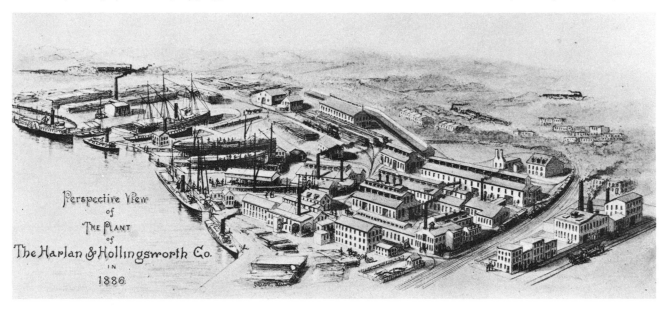

Perspective View
of
The Plant
of
The Harlan & Hollingsworth Co.
IN
1886.

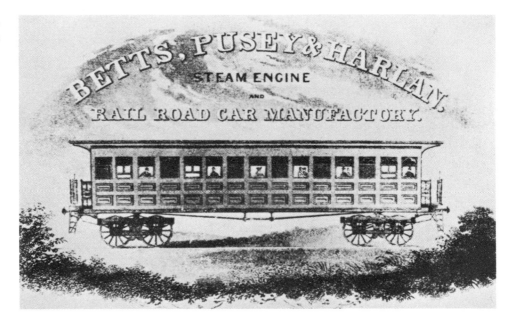

11. *Type of Railroad Cars Built by the Concern in 1836.* Early advertisement reproduced in *A Semi-Centennial Memoir of the Harlan & Hollingsworth Company,* opp. p. 193. (Courtesy E.M.H.L.)

parts of the country as at Philadelphia."[21] With these advantages, Harlan & Hollingsworth and Pusey & Jones were among the four largest builders of iron ships in the United States in 1880.[22] These two Wilmington companies used separate sales strategies. While the former sold most of their ships to New York shipping firms, the latter, looking farther afield, developed a lively trade with South America after a representative of the firm went to Brazil to study the Amazon so that the company could build iron riverboats designed to cope with that river's treacherous currents.[23]

Toward the end of the century when the center of car production shifted from the East to the Midwest, the Wilmington manufacturers increased

[21] U.S. Census, 1880, *Ship-Building Industry in the United States* (Washington, D.C., 1884), p. 208.

[22] U.S. Census, 1880, *Statistics of Manufactures* (Washington, D.C., 1883), 2:xxvi.

[23] *Every Evening,* Oct. 13, 1886.

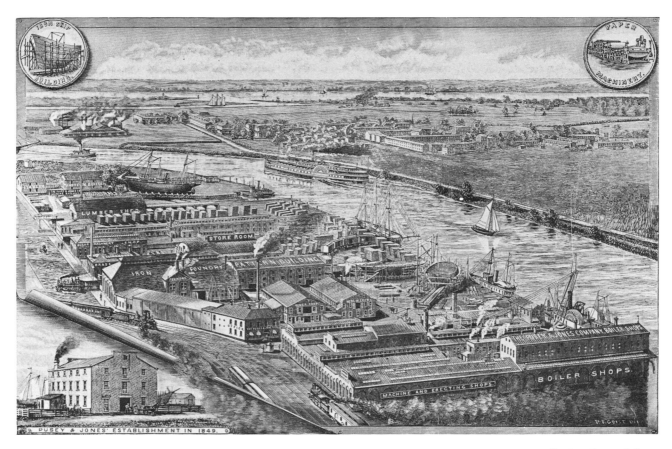

IRON SHIP BUILDING

PAPER MACHINERY

PUSEY & JONES' ESTABLISHMENT IN 1849.

their shipbuilding departments or sought other markets. The Pusey & Jones management, always on the lookout for product diversification in fields that required the highest level of the ironworker's skill, built up an important sideline in the manufacture of calender rolls for paper mills, which they sold both in the United States and in Europe.[24] Jackson & Sharp never entered the iron ship trade, but turned to trolley-car construction and became internationally known in that field.

Carriage making was another industry that blossomed in mid-century Wilmington. Like car building, carriage making required a variety of skilled workmen: upholsterers, carpenters, and painters. The industry would never have reached large proportions in Wilmington if the makers had been content to rely on local sales alone. Had they done so, the Wilmington carriage industry would have gone the way of Wilmington's boot and shoe manufacture, another consumer-oriented industry that yielded to more populous

12. *Bird's-Eye View of the Pusey & Jones Company*. Reproduced from George A. Wolf, *Industrial Wilmington* (Wilmington, 1898). (Courtesy E.M.H.L.)

[24] Thomas Savery Materials, accession no. 369, E.M.H.L.

13. *Samuel Harlan, Jr.* (*1808–1883*). Trained as a carpenter, Harlan was admitted to the firm of Betts, Pusey & Harlan in 1837 where he superintended the carbuilding shops. Reproduced from *A Semi-Centennial Memoir of the Harlan & Hollingsworth Company,* opp. p. 140. (Courtesy E.M.H.L.)

14. *Elijah Hollingsworth* (*1806–1866*). Born near Wilmington, Hollingsworth was a machinist with the Baldwin Locomotive Works before joining Betts, Pusey & Harlan in 1841. In 1849 Betts retired from the firm, which then became the Harlan & Hollingsworth Company. Reproduced from *A Semi-Centennial Memoir of the Harlan & Hollingsworth Company,* opp. p. 149. (Courtesy E.M.H.L.)

cities such as Philadelphia when factory techniques and inexpensive transportation pushed out the independent shops in smaller towns and cities. Instead, carriage making survived in Wilmington because manufacturers discovered a lucrative market for their product in southern states. Leading firms used the railroad to keep close contact with their southern markets, but shipped the carriages on coastal steamers to their showrooms in southern cities.[25] Wilmington's carriages were known for their elegance and careful construction, good selling points in the antebellum South. The heyday of Wilmington carriage making was in the 1850s and during the Civil War years when the carriage makers received lucrative government contracts for wagons and gun carriages. In 1864 McLear & Kendall, Wilmington's leading carriage builders, inaugurated the nation's first steam-powered carriage factory, described by a local writer as the largest in the United States.[26] In spite of this advance, the industry never really recovered from the Civil War because cheaper, cruder products flooded the market from Cincinnati and St. Louis shops in the postbellum period.

Tanning was another important industry in Wilmington. The city's advantages for this industry included large supplies of fresh water, the availability of tanning agents, and accessibility to international supplies of hides. Wilmington's tanneries turned out all the major specialties, from heavy cowhide belting to soft morocco kid for bookbindings and uppers for ladies' shoes. Many of the heavier hides tanned in Wilmington were sold locally for upholstery in railroad cars, luxury steamboats, and carriages. It was in the more delicate morocco trade, however, that Wilmington excelled, becoming after Philadelphia the largest producer of morocco in the United States. In 1890 Wilmington's manufactures were valued at over $4 million, Philadelphia's at $10 million.[27] Most of the hides used were imported from South America and Asia to Boston and New York, and then transshipped to the Delaware River's manufacturers by coastal ships.

By the 1850s Wilmington's economy had been transformed. The city directory for 1853 included tables of persons employed in the various major industries at that time. Two hundred and eighteen were listed as workers in

[25] *Harkness Magazine* 2 (1872): 120.
[26] *Ibid.*
[27] U.S. Census, 1890, *Manufacturing Industries* (Washington, D.C., 1895), 2:434–53, 618–19.

cotton manufacturing, 215 in the iron-casting trade, including wheel making, 675 worked in railroad-car manufacture and rolled iron and steel, 168 were employed in shipbuilding, 181 in carriage making, 178 in leather tanning, and 126 as coopers.[28] With the exception of the last named, these were the trades that continued to employ most of Wilmington's workmen through the remaining decades of the nineteenth century. The Civil War reinforced the trends already at work. Government orders for wagons and various leather goods encouraged expansion of the local carriage making and tanning industry, while the demands of a wartime economy benefitted the car makers, shipbuilders, and machine shops.

A notable aspect of the industrial pattern in Wilmington was the interrelationship among the local industries. The leather tanners sold considerable quantities of their products to carriage builders as upholstery material. The foundries turned out frames for carriages, parts for the machines, cars, boats, ships, and boilers that companies such as Pusey & Jones and Harlan & Hollingsworth fabricated. Wilmington's industrialists depended on Philadelphia for the importation of raw materials, either from abroad or, as in the case of coal and iron, from the interior of Pennsylvania, but Wilmington provided most of the processed goods for use in local manufacturing and raised its own investment capital. Important factors in Wilmington's successful adaptation to industrialization were her proximity to a major railroad line that linked her to the port of Philadelphia, southern markets for her manufactures, and nearby sources of iron and coal. An early tradition of milling on the Brandywine not only drew skilled mechanics to the area but also provided a market for the manufacture of machinery. Finally, the Christina River provided a waterway for coastal traffic in heavy raw materials and made possible the construction of small vessels more cheaply than in the larger Atlantic port cities.

[28] *Wilmington City Directory*, 1853, p. 74.

15. *A Sleeper for the Transcontinental Railroad.* Built by the Jackson & Sharp Company for the Central Pacific of California in 1869, the year that the transcontinental route was completed. (Courtesy E.M.H.L.)
16. *Nantucket Side-Wheeler.* Built in 1886 by the Pusey & Jones Company probably for the New Bedford, Martha's Vineyard and Nantucket Steamboat Co. (Courtesy E.M.H.L.)

The effects of the new industrial economy on Wilmington's growth pattern were steady rather than startling. The population rose from 8,452 in 1840 to 13,979 in 1850 and reached 21,508 by 1860, an increase of 67.1 percent in the latter decade alone. Population continued to grow at a rate of between 40 and 50 percent in each decade until the end of the century.[29]

The Factory System

The new industries profoundly altered the social structure of the community. The owners of the largest plants, mostly the sons of farmers or artisans, attained a level of wealth unmatched by the millers and merchants of previous generations. Industrialization made most workers, even those who were highly skilled, employees rather than masters.

The trend toward mechanization and larger industrial operating units transformed working conditions. Even skilled workmen lost control of their hours of labor and other aspects of their work. The characteristic size of early local industries—flour milling, shipbuilding, and coopering—was small. A master craftsman or owner worked with a few employees. As late as 1860 the largest of Wilmington's ten surviving cooper shops employed only sixteen workers.[30] Large numbers of workers were first used in water-powered industries—paper, gunpowder, and cotton mills—along the Brandywine. Upon visiting the Gilpin Paper Mill, Elizabeth Montgomery was amazed to see so many people at work in one place, "a large salle on the lower floor where more than 30 women were seated on high stools, at a long table placed before the windows, each one having a knife to pick the motes from every sheet."[31] Such a place was serene compared with the intensely active and noisy environments of the railroad-car shops. In the 1880s Jackson & Sharp's car plant employed a thousand men and had the capacity to build seventy to eighty cars at a time. As cars progressed toward completion, they were moved from building to building within the company's twenty-acre lot. An observer found that the most intriguing aspect of the

[29] U.S. Census, 1910, *Population* (Washington, D.C., 1913), 2:268.
[30] U.S. Census, 1860, New Castle County raw returns on microfilm, E.M.H.L.
[31] Montgomery, *Reminiscences*, p. 40.

17. *Constructing a Railroad Car.* Photographed ca. 1900 at the Jackson & Sharp Company.
(Courtesy E.M.H.L.)

29

process took place in the woodworking rooms. "In two immense rooms, which seem perfect wildernesses of machinery and ever-running, endless belts, innumerable wheels are whirring, and swift, steamdriven saws and blades are eating their way into oaken plank and beams. . . . The shrieking saws and rumbling planers make a wonderful conglomeration of noise. . . . In these great machinery halls there is no dust, for a complicated system of huge tubes ramifies throughout the building, and there is an open mouth at every piece of machinery, which sucks the sawdust. . . . they [the sawdust and bits of wood] are stored in a great brick stack contiguous to the boilers, and thus the waste of the mill is made to drive the engines which keep all of this machinery in motion."[32] In other rooms skilled upholsterers, carpenters, and painters put the finishing touches on parlor cars, coaches, sleepers, and privately commissioned cars. A visitor to the same plant a decade earlier was struck by the efficiency that characterized the assembly process. "First the visitor sees lumber in stock, a million feet of it; then, across one end of a long room, the mere sketch or transparent diagram of a car; then, a car broadly filled in; and soon, up to the last glorious result, upholstered with velvet and smelling of varnish. The cars are on rails, upon which they move, side on, as if by a principle of growth, the undeveloped ones perpetually pushing up their more forward predecessors."[33] Carriage making underwent a similar metamorphosis. Prior to the Civil War, carriage makers carried on their trade in relatively small shops using neither steam nor water power. John Merrick, owner of Wilmington's largest carriage manufactory, employed forty workmen in 1860; most others employed only a handful.[34] In the course of the next decade steam-powered machinery and larger production units were introduced into the carriage industry. In 1864 a new era began when the firm of McLear & Kendall moved into Merrick's new steam-powered factory, the largest and most modern in the United States at that time. The factory employed two hundred workmen and was capable of turning out forty-two carriages a week. Steam power was applied to the construction of carriages in such operations as woodcutting, jigsawing, planing, sanding, and boring holes. A visitor described the McLear & Ken-

[32] Scharf, *History of Delaware*, 2:774.
[33] *Lippincott's Magazine* (May 1877): 520.
[34] U.S. Census, 1860, New Castle County raw returns.

18. *An Assembly Line of Trolleys.* Photographed in 1899 at the Jackson & Sharp Company. (Courtesy E.M.H.L.)

dall shops in 1871 as "immense hives, swarming with industrious workers."[35]

Similarly in the leather industry, small tanyards gave way to large operations, although individual leather companies never grew to be as large as the car-building establishments. Already by 1858 a newspaper article reported that the Pusey & Scott morocco tannery was employing fifty-five workmen to turn out forty skins a day in a large three-story brick factory.[36] A twenty-four-horsepower steam engine moved the hides about in the tanning liquid to ensure uniform tanning. Otherwise the processes, such as removing hair and flesh from the hides, were done by hand. In another contemporary Wilmington tannery, Pyle, Wilson, & Pyle, a steam engine on the ground floor was used to pump tannin into the tanning vats. On the second floor men operated splitting machines, which cut the dried ox hides and thus enlarged the footage of usable hide surface. After this process, the hides were moved to the third floor for finishing, which the newspaper reporter described as "more interesting than pleasant, we could not help but think, on being ushered into close hot rooms where scarce a breath of fresh air and not a particle of dust must be allowed to enter . . . half-naked men flit about drawing from huge cupboard-like ovens the new baked sheets of leather. Coat after coat of the glossy varnish is now laid on; a week or two baking followed each successive coat until the sheets are made to shine like polished mirrors."[37] In 1872, when a reporter from the *Harkness Magazine* visited Pusey, Scott & Company morocco tannery, he saw "a bright room where ½ dozen pretty sewing machine girls are stitching the wet, slimy skins into bags" (for sumac) while "strong muscular Negroes" fill the bags with sumac dust and water in "gloomy cellars" and upstairs "young Swedes and Irish boys dress the dry skins, a backbreaking operation, apparently," commented the writer, "in the attitude of laundresses bent over an eternal washboard." The reporter further noted that Wilmington firms had pioneered in the introduction of labor-saving machines that minimized the need for men to handle the heavy skins.[38]

[35] *Harkness Magazine* 2:120–21.
[36] *Delaware State Journal*, May 28, 1858.
[37] *Ibid.*
[38] *Harkness Magazine*, 5:356.

During the 1880s and 1890s continued improvements in the leather industry brought additional changes. Firms that failed to adopt new equipment
went out of business; those that successfully met the challenge of technological improvement expanded. A local newspaper reported in 1898 that
"instead of the 100 firms turning out finished skins in this country 10 years
ago, there are now but 40. Then there were 1,500 people employed in
morocco factories of Wilmington, most of whom were men; now this industry means a living for 3,000 people, 1/3 of whom are women."[39] Women had
proved their ability to handle the glazing machines for polishing leather
that required much skill and strict attention. Because it was customary to
pay them considerably less than their male counterparts, women were sub-
stituted for male workers whenever possible. Tannery jobs that involved
hauling and lifting the heavy, moisture-soaked hides continued to employ
males, however.[40]

Large-scale mechanized production depended on the strict regulation of
employees. An example of the spirit that dominated Wilmington's factories
can be gleaned from the Lobdell Car Wheel Company work rules issued in
1841, which began: "The following rules will be strictly enforced. . . . There
must be system. . . . There is a place for everything and everything must be
in its place." Violators of rules were fined in varying amounts from a few
cents to a dollar. The work week was sixty hours in 1841, during which
employees were expected to be constantly attentive. "Any hand who is
found . . . standing about and talking unnecessarily" or "reading books or
newspapers during working hours" was subject to a twelve-and-a-half-cent
fine. Smokers were fined a dollar. The money collected provided a fund for
employees who "in the opinion of a majority of hands in the shop may at
any time stand in need of assistance." Each hand was provided with a book
or slate in which he kept a record of "the time he is employed in each job
of work," to be shown to the foreman on request.[41] Forty-five years later
at Harlan & Hollingsworth's, sixty hours still constituted the work week.
The workday began at 7:00 A.M. and ended at 6:00 P.M., with a midday
intermission of forty-five minutes for lunch. On Saturdays workers were

The Process of
Industrialization

[39] *Every Evening,* Feb. 3, 1898.
[40] *Ibid.*
[41] Accession no. 608, E.M.H.L.

19. *Workmen at Harlan & Hollingsworth Company.* A group photograph from *A Semi-Centennial Memoir of the Harlan & Hollingsworth Company,* opp. p. 318. (Courtesy E.M.H.L.)

released at 4:30 P.M. When the bell rang at 7:00 A.M., all employees were to be in their places ready to work. They were required to remain there until the bell rang to stop. "Any preparation for quitting, by washing of hands or otherwise, [was] positively forbidden." The timekeeper kept a record of everyone's arrival and departure. Once a week he tallied the total time of each employee in preparation for payday. The men were paid in cash each Tuesday. Reading, loitering, or unnecessary conversation during working hours was "positively prohibited," and "workmen running self-acting tools" were required to stay by their machines, and not go about the shop "interrupting others at their work. . . ."[42]

[42] *A Semi-Centennial Memoir of the Harlan & Hollingsworth Company* (Wilmington, Del., 1886), pp. 369–75.

34

Industrialization transformed Wilmington. Not only did population grow more rapidly than at any time in the city's history, from 8,000 in 1840 to 31,000 in thirty years, but the social fabric of the city was completely altered. No longer a town of merchants and independent artisans, wage-earning factory workers became the largest single occupational category in the city's economy. The 1880 census revealed that 44.4 percent of Wilmington's work force was engaged in manufactures; only 10 percent of the total work force held white-collar jobs.[43] The city's industrial potential attracted new ethnic groups to the community. By 1870 one-fifth of Wilmington's population was foreign-born, mostly Irish and German.[44] Wilmington had become a city of varied industries, mostly owned and managed by residents of the city who had become the wealthiest and most powerful members of the community.

[43] U.S. Census, 1880, *Statistics of Manufactures*, 2:206.
[44] U.S. Census, 1870, *Population and Social Statistics* (Washington, D.C., 1872), 1:97.

CHAPTER II

The Dynamics of Physical Growth: Politics and Utilities

Urbanization

Drastic changes in the physical configuration of the city accompanied industrialization. Eighteenth-century Wilmington had been a collection of houses and shops arranged in a grid pattern around Market Street facing the docks and shipyards on the Christina River. Nearby to the north was a smaller cluster of homes, mills, and cooper shops at Brandywine Village. In the 1840s and 1850s industrial concentration along the Christina increased the density of settlement in that area and began the twofold process of segregation of habitation from place of work and of working-class housing from middle- and upper-middle-class housing that Sam B. Warner discovered in Philadelphia.[1] These processes were exacerbated in Wilmington by the peculiarities of the configuration of the land. On either side of the Christina and particularly on the east side of Market Street the lands are flat, low-lying, and even marshy in places, while the land on the west side slowly rises to a high point that marks the watershed between the Brandywine and Christina, running along the course of modern-day Delaware Avenue westward from Tenth and Market streets. The high and healthful west side, more suitable as a residential area, attracted middle- and upper-middle-class home builders. Meanwhile, developers of working-class housing built row upon row of speculative two-story brick homes for the working class on the low, flat east side near the factory district.[2]

The introduction of a horse trolley line and of large-scale commercial land development in the 1860s solidified the emerging pattern of residential

[1] Warner, *The Private City*, pp. 49–62.
[2] Richard Clark, "Plan of the City of Wilmington—1850," Special Collections, H.M.M.L.

---

20. *The South Millrace in Brandywine Park* has supplied water to the pumping station since 1826. The Van Buren Street Bridge, built in 1908, was a joint project of the street and sewer department and the water department designed to carry a large water pipe from the Porter Reservoir on the Concord Pike. (Courtesy H.S.D.)

21. *Joshua T. Heald* (*1821–1887*). Portrait from the *Historical and Biographical Encyclopaedia of Delaware* (Wilmington, 1882), opp. p. 569. (Courtesy E.M.H.L.)

38

clustering. The man most responsible for these innovations was Joshua T. Heald, a Quaker farm boy who came to Wilmington in search of a business career and became in turn a shopkeeper, conveyancer, and land developer.[3] Heald was Wilmington's most dynamic and effective booster in the 1860s and 1870s. He envisioned the city as a great rail terminus as well as a center for industry. His real estate ventures formed only one part of an elaborate personal plan for the city's development, which called for the construction of two new railroad lines designed to tap the Pennsylvania coal fields and western trade, and for extensive improvements to the harbor at the confluence of the Delaware and Christina rivers.

In 1867 Heald was also the prime mover in creating the Wilmington board of trade, an association of men engaged in both manufacturing and commercial pursuits and dedicated to the proposition that "men and not natural advantages make great and prosperous cities."[4] The board lobbied unsuccessfully to improve Wilmington's passenger train service, to reduce telegraph charges, and to secure the repeal of Delaware's usury law. It also lent support to Heald's railroad and real estate ventures in the hope of transforming Wilmington into an important east coast port and rail center.[5] Although Heald's dream of making Wilmington a powerful commercial city was thwarted by Philadelphia's far greater commercial resources, his land use plans had a decisive effect on the pattern of the city's development.

In 1860 Heald was made the agent for the division and sale of lots from the Shallcross farm property, a 176-acre tract located northwest of the built-up portion of the city adjacent to the Brandywine. Heald conceived of the tract, the largest yet to be offered for housing in Wilmington, as a prestige residential area, but he recognized that suburban development depended on regular, rapid transportation into the center of town. Therefore Heald formed the Wilmington City Railway Company which laid tracks from the PW&BRR Station at Front and French streets up Market Street to Tenth

[3] J. M. McCarter and B. F. Jackson, eds., *Historical and Biographical Encyclopaedia of Delaware* (Wilmington, Del., 1882), pp. 569–71.

[4] Monte A. Calvert, "The Wilmington Board of Trade, 1867–1875," *Delaware History* 12 (1967): 179.

[5] *Ibid.*, pp. 175–97.

22. House of Colonel Henry McComb. Eleventh Street between Market and King streets. The house, which together with its grounds occupied an entire block, was demolished to make way for the Federal Building in the 1930s. (Courtesy E.M.H.L.)

and out Delaware Avenue past the Shallcross property.[6] The horsecars began rolling at ten-minute intervals in the summer of 1864, and in its first year the line carried 450,000 people at six cents per fare.[7] The car line had just the effect Heald had anticipated, for in the course of the next two decades Wilmington's wealthiest citizens erected mansions along Delaware Avenue, making its environs the most prestigious residential section of the city.

During these same years Heald was also engaged in the real estate development of the east side. In 1866 he created the Christiana River Improve-

[6] *Delaware State Journal*, July 1, 1864.
[7] *Ibid.*, July 14, 1865.

23. *Residence of Job H. Jackson.* Occupied the site on Delaware Avenue between Washington and Jefferson streets where the YMCA building now stands. Note the attempt to create a country park setting in the city. (Courtesy E.M.H.L.)

ment Company for the purpose of promoting the maximum utilization of lands along the river. The company engaged in dredging and land-fill operations and bought unused land for the purpose of selling it for the erection of factories, commercial wharves, and working-class homes. Acting sometimes through the Christiana Improvement Company and sometimes as an independent real estate agent, Heald built many rows of working-class housing in this low, marshy region. Also in 1866 he bought a large tract south of the Christina River Bridge at Third Street where he erected rows of brick homes located to appeal to the men who were employed at various riverside factories in that area. Known locally as "over Third Street Bridge" or South Wilmington, the neighborhood soon acquired an unsavory reputa-

41

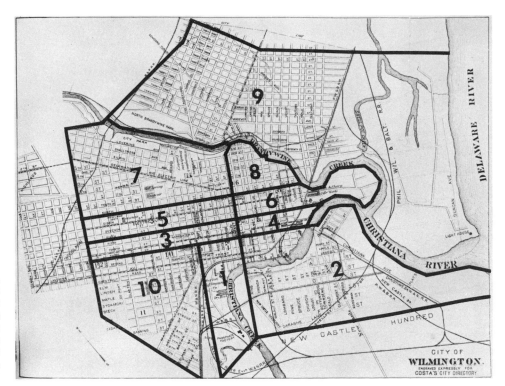

Maps 3 and 4. The map, taken from the *Wilmington City Directory,* 1892, has been marked to show the changes in the composition of the city's wards between the 1880 and 1890 censuses as shown in Table 1. (Courtesy E.M.H.L.)

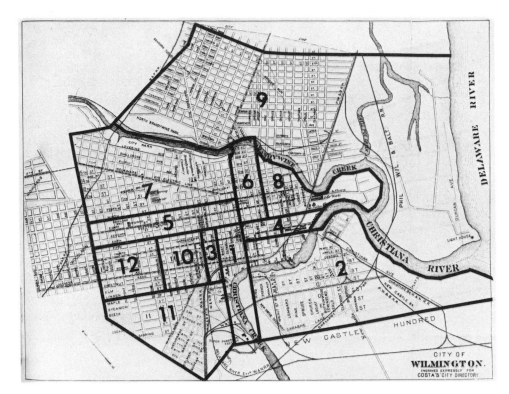

tion. Those who could afford better housing avoided South Wilmington because drainage there was very poor, a real health hazard in the age of backyard privies. Another Heald development in northeast Wilmington near the Brandywine was similarly plagued. The Christina River Valley offered excellent industrial sites but was inappropriate for residential use, yet nineteenth-century economic realities—especially the need for workers to live within walking distance of their jobs—imposed poor housing locations on many working-class Wilmingtonians.

Table 1. Growth of population, by wards

Ward	1870	1880	1890	1900	1910
1	5,505	3,080	2,786	3,041	2,645
2	2,942	4,267	5,240	5,560	5,201
3	2,991	3,790	5,153	5,375	5,441
4	3,881	3,871	4,030	4,037	3,818
5	3,990	5,475	7,408	8,966	10,025
6	5,523	4,034	5,356	6,061	6,040
7	3,009	5,320	8,651	12,816	14,980
8	1,584	5,442	8,244	8,848	9,010
9	1,416	2,272	4,624	7,304	10,601
10		4,927	5,016	6,409	6,653
11			2,498	3,800	6,811
12			2,425	4,291	6,186

SOURCES: U.S. Census, 1870, *Population and Social Statistics*, 1:97; 1880, *Population*, 1:417; 1890, *Population*, 1:526; 1900, *Population*, 1:650; 1910, *Population*, 2:283.

The city's expansion put a severe strain on the one public utility then available, water, and drew attention to the need for additional services such as sewers, parks, and paved streets. The city government, however, was ill-designed to undertake projects that required heavy capitalization and constant administration. The dilemma inherent in this situation created the city's chief political battleground in the late nineteenth century with upper-middle-class industrialists often pitted against the conservative-minded politicians. In spite of the many obstacles that threatened to block efforts to increase the responsibility of the public sector in commu-

24. *Working-Class Housing on Christiana Street.* Photograph, ca. 1930, showing decayed houses in southwest Wilmington typical of working-class houses erected in the city during the middle and late nineteenth century. Photograph by Frank Zebley.

25. *Middle Depot Car Barn, Delaware Avenue and DuPont Street.* An undated photograph, ca. 1880, showing a team of horses about to pull a trolley out of the barn. (Courtesy E.M.H.L.)

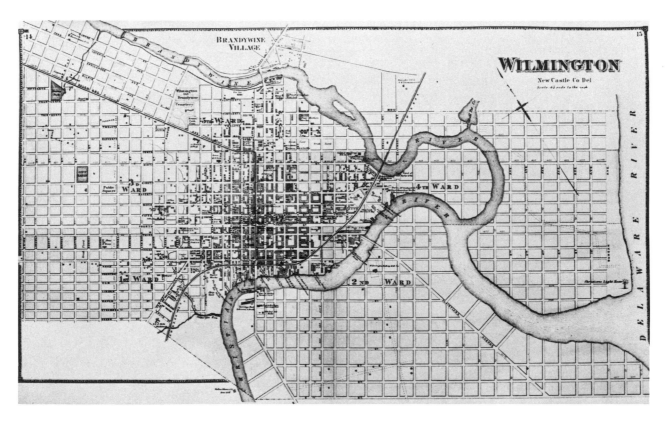

Map 5. Wilmington. *Pomeroy and Beer's New Topographical Atlas of the State of Delaware* (Philadelphia, 1868), p. 14. This map shows the Wilmington City Railway Line, which ran west on Front Street from the P.W.&B. Station to Market, north on Market to Tenth and out Delaware Avenue. Note the Shallcross property in the upper left-hand corner bounded by Delaware Avenue, Wilmington and Brandywine Cemetery and the Brandywine River. Note also the plans for extensive additions to the city toward the Delaware River on land that was as yet undeveloped and poorly drained. (Courtesy E.M.H.L.)

nity life, the advocates of the utilities had triumphed on every issue they raised before the century's end. And although these victories were not won without considerable cost to the integrity of the democratic process, the entire community was much enriched by public improvements that made the city a more healthful, more pleasant, and in short, more humane environment in which to live.

The need for additional sources of fresh water gave the initial impetus to the city government's involvement in utilities. In 1810 it took over the responsibility for water supply when the burgesses bought out a private spring water company that had been piping water throughout the town to supplement the inadequate supplies from private wells.[8] Having assumed responsibility for water supply, the burgesses faced increasing problems as population expanded beyond the capacity of the city's springs to meet the demand. At first the town fathers tried palliative measures. On the theory that the roots of the Lombardy poplars and willows along the city streets were clogging the pipes, they ordered the trees removed over the angry protests of many tree lovers.[9] When this controversial action produced no positive results, the burgesses were forced to conclude that they must tap some new source of water. Using Benjamin Latrobe's famed Philadelphia Water Works as a model, the city purchased a gristmill on the Brandywine in 1827 as well as a square of property at the crest of the hill that separates the Brandywine drainage area from the Christina River Valley. Water was pumped through iron pipes from the mill to a reservoir on the hilltop property from which gravity carried water to the households, fireplugs, and cisterns below. This, the city's first major public work, was completed at a cost of $42,026.00.[10]

In the 1830s after considerable agitation by Wilmington lawyers and business leaders who wished to transfer jurisdiction over local criminal cases from the county seat at New Castle to Wilmington, the state legislature granted Wilmington a new city charter that replaced the burgesses with a mayor-council plan of government. The form of the new government reflected its drafters' preoccupation with the addition of a mayor's court.

[8] Scharf, *History of Delaware,* 2:664–65.

[9] Montgomery, *Reminiscences,* pp. 230–31.

[10] Scharf, *History of Delaware,* 2:665. The reservoir was on the site of the present-day Rodney Square between Market and King streets and Tenth and Eleventh streets.

26. *Delaware Avenue in the 1890s,* looking eastward from Franklin Street. This tree-lined street was Wilmington's principal showplace. Note the granite and brick paving. (Courtesy H.S.D.)

Wilmington,
Delaware

The hallmark of the charter was the creation of the office of mayor, but the mayor was conceived as a peace officer and judge rather than as an executive. He was empowered to appoint a constabulary force, to preside over the mayor's court, and to appoint the board of health. All other municipal functions were relegated to the city council, composed of elected representatives from the various city wards, which was organized as a legislative body, not an executive one.[11]

The mayor-council plan, as adopted by Wilmington in 1832, proved to be an awkward organization for the administration of public services because it provided no focal point for executive responsibility. It was unclear whether the administration of public services came under the authority of the various committees of the city council or of the council as a whole. Furthermore, the council, made up of representatives of contending political parties, could not approach problems as a unified body. In most years about a half of the councilmen were skilled workers—machinists, carpenters, tailors, and the like—most of the remaining members being owners of small manufactories or of retail establishments. These men took part in politics because it afforded them personal satisfaction and status, but they were not men of broad vision, were easily diverted into petty partisanship, and were eager to hold down expenses since their principal campaign device was to characterize the opposition as spendthrifts. In Wilmington the two parties fought a see-saw battle for political control, with the Democrats depending on the immigrant vote and on migrants from rural southern Delaware and Maryland, while the Republicans' support came from business leaders and, after the Civil War, from blacks.[12]

The Need for Services

The organization of Wilmington's government and the preoccupations of its politicians became more than an academic concern when council failed to take the initiative in solving problems of the growing city's water supply

[11] *Ibid.,* p. 640.
[12] David P. Peltier, "Nineteenth-Century Voting Patterns in Delaware," *Delaware History* 13 (1969): 228.

48

and sewage disposal. Expansion into the higher western portion of the city rendered the old water system installed in the 1820s hopelessly inadequate. West-side residents discovered that their water pressure was always low and that sometimes they could get no water at all during business hours when industries were draining off the meager supply. Simultaneously, physicians editorialized in the press about the increasing industrial pollution of the Brandywine.[13] During a typhoid epidemic in the late 1840s eighty-nine people died. The usual death rate from that disease was about fourteen per year in the 1860s, and most deaths occurred in the poorly drained east side. Diphtheria and cholera were also deadly, the latter killed

[13] *Wilmington Daily Commercial,* Feb. 14, 1867.

27. *Mills and Pumping Station on the Brandywine.* The water pumping station is shown toward the right in this undated photograph, probably taken in the 1880s. (Courtesy W.I.F.L.)

an average of thirty-three Wilmingtonians a year in the 1870s.[14] As the pressures mounted, the city council demonstrated its inability to take action. In 1870 the council rejected its own water committee's recommendations for an improved supply system because some members feared both the high cost and the possible patronage payoffs to political opponents.[15]

In 1871 the Republican-controlled council attempted to resolve the problem by creating the office of chief engineer and thus fixing responsibility for water supply on one man. Their appointee was C. H. Gallagher, formerly a Republican member of the watering committee.[16] Three years later when depression struck the country, the council had taken no further action. Gallagher seized upon the depression as an opportunity for the city to build a west-side reservoir at reduced cost, while simultaneously repaying the party faithful by giving them jobs. The Democrats on the council naturally objected to Gallagher's plan. Some Republican members also distrusted his motives. They foresaw the rise of a machine replete with boss rule if the reservoir were to be built with patronage labor and accused him of being at the center of a ring.[17] The city council agreed to appropriate funds to begin the reservoir, but anti-Gallagher councilmen were sufficiently powerful to force the water department to contract out for most of the work.[18] Shortly thereafter the council replaced Gallagher with a less ambitious chief, but the reservoir itself continued to be a politically charged issue.[19] In 1875 when the Democrats won control of the city council, they removed the Republican water chief for yet a third man. In the meanwhile more time and energy were wasted investigating and castigating the various water chiefs than was spent building the reservoir. The fact that neither party could maintain power in the council led to constant bickering and maneuvering for advantage over every measure that arose

[14] L. P. Bush, *Some Vital Statistics of the City of Wilmington* (Wilmington, Del., 1877), pamphlet, W.I.F.L.

[15] *Wilmington Daily Commercial*, Sept. 15, 1871.

[16] C. H. Gallagher, *Annual Report of the Chief Engineer of the Water Department* (Wilmington, Del., 1872), p. 111.

[17] *Every Evening*, July 17, 18, 1874.

[18] *Ibid.*, July 24, 31, 1874.

[19] *Ibid.*, Oct. 2, 1874; Nov. 14, 1874.

regarding the project. By the spring of 1877, after the city had spent three hundred thousand dollars on the reservoir, it was still nowhere near completion.[20]

At this point a group of discontented west-side residents, business and professional men, petitioned the state legislature to create a special commission to supervise the reservoir project.[21] The success of their petition began a radical change in the government of the city and ushered in a period of remarkable progress in a wide range of public services. The Democratic state legislature was naturally willing to undermine the patronage power of the usually Republican city council. In 1877 the legislators adopted a bill to permit the city to borrow an additional hundred and fifty thousand dollars toward the completion of the reservoir, with the stipulation that the project must be administered by an ad hoc commission of three qualified, nonpartisan men who had been suggested to the legislature by the petitioners. The commissioners moved the reservoir project forward and completed the first of two basins before the year was out.[22] The city council, furious at being deprived of control over a municipal undertaking, complained that the democratic process was being subverted; but there was nothing illegal in the state legislature's action, and it proved to be successful from a pragmatic point of view.

Underlying the commission movement were antagonisms based on differences of class and life-style. Supporters of the commission were convinced that most councilmen were incompetent to organize and manage a large-scale enterprise. The evidence seemed incontrovertible. For example, in 1871 the city's leading physicians had applied for a charter to begin a private hospital for victims of industrial accidents, but the city council decided that the city should provide a public hospital instead.[23] Since the city required only one hospital, the physicians dropped their project and most of them refused to treat patients in the city facility, which they re-

[20] *Ibid.,* Apr. 14, 1877.
[21] *Ibid.,* Mar. 20, 21, 1877.
[22] *Ibid.,* Dec. 15, 1877.
[23] D. W. Maull, *A Municipal Hospital, A Necessity* (Wilmington, Del., 1873), pamphlet, W.I.F.L.

garded as a political boondoggle rather than a medical unit.[24] The councilmen not only proved to be inept administrators, they also padded the institution's expenses to provide fancy dinners for themselves, and the hospital was quietly abandoned amid a barrage of attacks from the press.[25] Since
the majority of councilmen were craftsmen and retailers in small stores,
they were accustomed to close personal relationships with their employees or fellow workers. The men who had pressed for the water commission and those who were chosen to serve on it were, by contrast, accustomed
to working out problems involving the allocation of large sums of money
and dealing with many employees in an impersonal manner. When councilmen charged the commission with the usurpation of democratic government, there was an underlying resentment of men who recognized that the
city's wealthier and more prominent citizens distrusted their stewardship.
When the commission supporters, on the other hand, pleaded for a business approach to municipal government, they had in mind the creation of
an apolitical administration similar to those that governed their own occupations.[26]

In pressing for more utilities the business leaders of Wilmington demonstrated that while they were unwilling to become directly involved in politics as elected public officials, neither were they abrogating their duties as
community leaders. Their involvement was motivated by a peculiar blend
of altruism and self-interest. These men lived in the city, not in distant
suburbs. If the city was unhealthy, dirty, and ugly, they could escape these
conditions only a bit better than an east-side working man. Furthermore,
in the years following the panic of 1873, Wilmington's economic future appeared less bright than in the fifties and sixties. Several of the city's key industries were encountering stiff competition. Carriage building never revived after the war, and the city's car-building shops, which led the nation
in the early seventies, could not compete with George Pullman's Illinois-
based car works in securing contracts from western railroads. After the
debacle of 1873 ended Wilmington's commercial hopes, the city's board of
trade concentrated its efforts on attracting new industry.[27] The board

[24] *Every Evening,* Sept. 25, 1878.
[25] *Ibid.,* Oct. 25, 1879.
[26] *Ibid.,* Apr. 21, 1883.
[27] *Annual Report Wilmington Board of Trade* (Wilmington, Del., 1873), E.M.H.L.

members thought that an important consideration in relocating industries would be the healthfulness and attractiveness of their proposed surroundings. A city that projected a sense of progress had parks, sewers, and paved streets. They believed that only if Wilmington acquired these improvements could the city have a bright future.

The growing conviction that man could limit the ravages of disease was another reason why business and professional leaders supported utilities. In 1881 a smallpox epidemic struck Wilmington. In a single year the death rate rose from 21.20 to 28.83 per thousand. The board of health blamed the deaths on the contamination of the city's drinking water. The board cautioned that "with the light which of late years has been thrown upon the subject of preventable diseases, the board is well satisfied that many attacks of serious disease, and in some cases deaths, have resulted from defective plumbing in our city. . . . The sewerage in our city is not only defective but is scandalous. . . . Unless some proper system of sewerage is adopted, a terrible penalty of disease and death awaits the people of the city."[28] Both the board of trade and city council responded to this strongly voiced criticism. Prodded by the board, the city council after years of procrastination finally took the lead and hired a sanitary engineer who surveyed Wilmington's sanitation needs and reported that the problems of water contamination and sewerage were intimately connected. The Brandywine, he said, was not only polluted by mills upstream from the city but by the drainage from cesspools, a cemetery, and factories within the city itself. The engineer therefore urged the city to construct an intercepting sewer along the section of the Brandywine that was subject to this urban pollution as the first priority in the creation of a complete sewerage system.[29]

The board of trade was equally concerned about the effects of sewage on the Christina River. In 1880 a committee from the board met with representatives of the U.S. Army Engineers to discuss the possibility of federal aid to dredge the silt-filled river. According to the local press, the engineer in charge of the Philadelphia region had castigated the city for its own indifference to the cause of silting and had told the committee members that

[28] *Annual Report of the Board of Health* (Wilmington, Del., 1881).
[29] Rudolph Hering, *Report on a System of Sewerage for the City of Wilmington* (Wilmington, Del., 1883).

28. *Dredging in the Christina River.* An undated photograph from the Jackson & Sharp Collection. (Courtesy E.M.H.L.)

the U.S. Government "would not become a scavenger of the city." If Wilmington was to continue as a shipbuilding center "the city [must] trap, or otherwise protect the stream from city washings and the offal of the manufacturies. Wilmington has reached the stage in its development when it is necessary to abandon primitive methods [of sewage disposal], take advantage of the accumulated knowledge of all civilized countries and adopt suitable precautions to preserve both the integrity of its river and the health of its people." He concluded with the warning that "the interest and action of the U.S. Government in the matter of the Christina navigation are subordinate to, and must, I should say, depend upon the interest and action of the city of Wilmington."[30]

The experts agreed and the board of trade was convinced. In its annual report of 1882, the board declared that cesspools were slowly poisoning the

[30] *Every Evening,* Jan. 19, 1881.

54

soil of Wilmington and causing such illnesses as typhoid fever, diphtheria, consumption, and cholera.[31]

It was the practice then in Wilmington to employ an odorless excavator company to clean the cesspools. This costly and cumbersome process of sewage removal worked reasonably well on the west-side hills, but it did not prevent the drainage of organic wastes into the lower land on the east side where basements reaked of the stench.[32]

Having tried the commission method successfully once before, advocates of utilities turned to it again. In 1883 when the state legislature was persuaded to create a permanent bipartisan water commission, the mugwumpish Democrat *Every Evening* editorialized, "It may be safely said that two-

[31] *Ibid.,* Mar. 1, 1882.
[32] *Annual Report of the Street and Sewer Department* (Wilmington, Del., 1892).

29. *Looking North on Market Street from the Christina River.* Undated photograph taken probably in the 1870s or 1880s when Market Street was still paved in cobblestones. The hill directed drainage into the river. (Courtesy H.S.D.)

thirds of the businessmen of the city, without regard to party, are better
satisfied to have the water department in the hands of the very able and practically nonpartisan commission appointed, than managed by a notoriously
incompetent council."[33] Even the Republican *Morning News* acquiesced.[34]
The commissioners, named in the act, were empowered to appoint their
own successors at the conclusion of their terms.[35] The legislature thus
placed them beyond the control of the regular channels of city government.

In the 1880s when municipal improvements were the liveliest political
issue in Wilmington, the most significant pressure group supporting the
utilities was the board of trade, which represented the city's industrial and
commercial leaders. The board members were united in their belief that
Wilmington must have sewerage and street paving, but they were also convinced that the city government as presently constituted could neither build
nor administer these improvements. Rather than petition the legislature for
a new city charter with a strong executive, an appeal that was sure to en-
counter grave difficulties since it involved a loss of the legislature's powers,
the board chose to work for immediate solutions to the utilities problem.

In February 1887 the sewerage issue approached the point of resolution
when a private company offered the city a thirty-year contract to build and
administer sewers. Interested citizens, invited to meet in the board of trade
rooms to discuss the offer, decided that the city could save money as well as
retain local control if Wilmington constructed sewers at its own expense.[36]
The meeting appointed a bipartisan committee to devise a plan to expedite
the project. The committee led by J. Parke Postles, prominent among the
city's tanners, proposed a bipartisan commission similar to the water commission. City council, of course, opposed the creation of yet another commission, but it was in a poor position to press its case with either the legislature or the public because of an embarrassing deficit in the city's finances
due to the council's overzealous tax-cutting.[37] Postles, speaking for the
board of trade, admitted in testimony before a legislative committee that

[33] *Every Evening,* Apr. 21, 1883.
[34] *Morning News,* Mar. 10, 1883.
[35] *Ibid.,* Apr. 26, 1883.
[36] *Every Evening,* Feb. 16, 1887.
[37] *Ibid.,* Mar. 26, 1887.

the commission bill should be considered a stopgap rather than a permanent solution to Wilmington's municipal problems. He viewed the passage of this bill as a step toward the adoption of a comprehensive revision of the city's charter in which the city council would become a legislative body and the mayor would be the chief executive officer of the city in charge of municipal services. But, he argued, just because such a plan was politically unfeasible at present, the city should not postpone the construction of sewers.[38] The legislature passed the bill a few days later.[39]

Unlike the water commission, which inherited a functioning system, the street and sewer commissioners began with little. Approximately 128 of the city's 150 miles of street were not paved at all, but merely covered with rubble. Fourteen miles of street surface were paved in cobblestone, which was hard on horses' hooves, "noisy, dusty, and otherwise disagreeable."[40] In wet weather the streets were as deep in mud as country roads and "pitted with muddy hollows."[41] If the streets were in poor condition, the sewers were nonexistent except for a few that were privately owned. The most pressing need was for an intercepting sewer along the Brandywine to prevent contamination of the water supply. This project, which had been the highlight of the sanitary engineer's report in 1883, became the top priority for the new board.

With the further support of the board of trade, the state legislature adopted an act in 1891 to finance streets and sewers by charging the owners of adjacent properties two-thirds of the cost of these improvements.[42] Having eliminated the problem of cost, the commissioners moved swiftly to fulfill their charge. Their engineer's survey of the city's sewerage needs concluded that geographical variations posed an obstacle to their ultimate goal of a citywide sewer system. "Our city is largely built upon a hill with a large flat area at the foot, which area is unfortunately the most densely populated portion of the city," he reported, "and the residents, as it generally happens in all manufacturing cities, are not able financially to protect themselves

[38] *Ibid.*, Apr. 12, 1887.
[39] *Ibid.*, Apr. 16, 21, 1887.
[40] *Ibid.*, May 17, 1875.
[41] *Ibid.*, Feb. 19, 1883.
[42] *Annual Report of the Street and Sewer Department* (Wilmington, Del., 1891), pp. 107–8.

30. *Shipley Run Sewer,*
Under Maryland Avenue.
Taken from the *8th Annual*
Report of the Board of
Directors of the Street and
Sewer Department of Wil-
mington, Delaware (Wil-
mington, 1895). A major
priority in the department
was the construction of large
sewers such as this to
channel streams already
polluted by factories and
privies. (Courtesy
H.M.M.L.)

from the evils of sewage pollution as their neighbors living on the higher
elevations. . . ."[43] The various elevations required the installation of different
types of sewers. Because it was cheaper to lay sewers in the high lands than
in the low, where pumps were required, it is not surprising that the initial
stages of sewer construction were in the northwest portion of the city, beginning with the long-proposed intercepting sewer along the Brandywine.
By 1896, 47.63 miles of sewer line had been laid, emptying into the Delaware
River.[44] It was not until the turn of the century, however, that the department undertook to build sewers in the Christina lowlands, some parts of
which the commission's engineer described as "absolutely uninhabitable for
American citizens because of no drainage."[45]

The department pursued an equally ambitious program of street paving.
With a variety of paving materials to choose from, the board decided to

[43] *Ibid.*, 1892, p. 119.
[44] *Ibid.*, 1896, p. 3.
[45] *Ibid.*, 1899, p. 46.

vary materials in accordance with the traffic patterns of the city. Granite blocks were laid on those downtown streets which sustained the heaviest traffic, macadam was used in residential areas, and brick surfaces were laid in sections of middling traffic.[46] By the mid-nineties Wilmington's appearance was transformed by nine miles of granite, six miles of brick, and thirteen miles of macadam surfaces. Just as the depression in the 1870s expedited the reservoir project, the depression years of the nineties created a favorable labor market. The commissioners, at some pains to show that politics had no place in their hiring practices, asked charitable groups for the names of jobless men and alternated work gangs in an effort to spread the work to as many men as possible.[47]

Parks were another important symbol of urban progress in the late nineteenth century. In Wilmington, agitation for a public park began in the 1860s when the city's expansion posed a threat to the favorite local picnic

[46] *Ibid.,* 1895, p. 7.
[47] *Ibid.,* p. 8.

31. *West Front Street— Granite Block Paving.* Note the reliance on hand labor rather than machines. Taken from the *11th Annual Statement of the Board of Directors of the Street and Sewer Department of Wilmington, Delaware* (Wilmington, 1898). (Courtesy H.M.M.L.)

area along the southeast side of the Brandywine adjacent to Heald's Shall-cross development. Heald himself was eager to see these woods developed as a park. His advocacy led to the creation of a committee of leading citizens chaired by U.S. Senator Thomas F. Bayard to study the proposal. The committeemen, charmed by the idea of a Brandywine Park, drew up an elaborate plan for the site, including a playground "with mazes and labyrinths, miniature lakes pleasant for rowing in the summer and skating in the winter" and even a small zoo.[48] They reported enthusiastically that a park would raise land values throughout the city and would help to improve "the culture, taste and morals of the community." "Those who have faith in the future of Wilmington . . . expect to see here a large and thickly populated city," they said. "Even now, in all the built up portions of the town, we have not a single Public Square, not a place where the mothers with their children, or the aged people can stroll, away from the noise and dust of the city, without being trespassers." The plan failed to generate much enthusiasm among the citizenry, many of whom feared that a park would mean higher taxes, and the proposal had to be put aside.[49]

Parks again became a public issue in the early 1880s when William P. Bancroft, a son of Joseph Bancroft the textile manufacturer, offered Wilmington an eighty-acre tract of land along the Brandywine on the condition that the city add more contiguous land and administer the park through a nonpartisan commission.[50] Bancroft initiated his drive to secure a public park by inviting a number of influential citizens both in and out of government to informal meetings. At the first meeting Mayor John P. Wales, George H. Bates, a prominent attorney, Joshua T. Heald, William M. Canby, president of the Wilmington Savings Fund Society and a city councilman from the silk stocking Seventh Ward, Colonel Henry A. du Pont and J. Taylor Gause, president of Harlan & Hollingsworth were constituted a committee to plan how the city might acquire a public park. The committee drafted a commission bill for the state legislature and sponsored a public meeting, attended by only twenty-five persons, to secure broad-

---

[48] *Report of A Committee of Citizens to the City Council on the Subject of a Public Park for the City of Wilmington* (Wilmington, Del., 1869), p. 5.
[49] *Wilmington Daily Commercial*, June 3, 1868. *Report of the Board of Park Commissioners, 1895* (Wilmington, Del., 1896), p. 10.
[50] *Report of the Board of Park Commissioners, 1895*, p. 14.

32. *William Poole Bancroft* (*1835–1928*). A Quaker philanthropist. (Courtesy H.S.D.)

61

based citizen support for the measure.[51] It was not the "general public" but the industrial magnates who exhibited interest and willingness to pay higher city taxes to acquire public parks. J. T. Gause, one of the city's richest and least sentimental citizens, wrote a letter to the editor of the *Every Evening* expressing his view: "I have watched to find the objections to the park scheme, and have yet to hear of but the single one, of increased taxation. If this consideration had been uppermost in the past we would never have had our water supply, our public schoolhouses, and the many other public improvements that have gone so far to make our city what it is." He contended that the largest taxpayers in the city were united in support of the park proposal.[52]

The park commission bill was passed with ease and the commissioners, who included William P. Bancroft among their number, set out to develop a comprehensive park program for Wilmington. In a wise public relations move, they invited Frederick Law Olmsted, the famed creator of New York's Central Park, to study the Brandywine site. His ecstatic report published in the local press aided their drive to secure additional parkland.[53] Recognizing that parks and playgrounds were needed in the densely settled areas of the city as well as in the more fashionable district near Brandywine Park, the board established several small parks in various parts of the city, including the east side. By 1895, just a decade after the board commenced its work, the city could boast 252 square acres of parkland, which averaged out to one acre of parkland to every 25½ acres of city land, or one acre of parkland to every 270 inhabitants.[54]

After the initial stage of acquiring land, the board turned its attention to the creation of recreation facilities. With its limited budget, nothing like the splendor suggested by the 1869 report on Brandywine Park was possible, but some improvements, such as the addition of drives, benches, swimming pools, and a small zoo were realized by 1900. Swimming pools and organized summer playgrounds were an important innovation at the turn of the century. In 1898, its first year, the pool in Brandywine Park attracted over 24,000 male and 1,000 female bathers.[55] In subsequent years, pools were

---

[51] *Every Evening*, Feb. 24, 1883.
[52] *Ibid.*, June 2, 1886.
[53] *Ibid.*, June 26, 1885.
[54] *Report of the Board of Park Commissioners*, 1895, p. 2.   [55] *Ibid.*, 1898.

33. *A Winter Scene.* Ice skating in Brandywine Park, from *The Board of Park Commissioners Annual Report for the Year Ending December 31, 1896* (Wilmington, 1897).

34. *Pine Street Playground.* Supervised play in a city park from *The Board of Park Commissioners Annual Report for the Year Ending December 31, 1908* (Wilmington, 1909).

built in other city parks, including those on the east side. In 1909 the board experimented with organized play, centering on games and crafts for white children at the Pine Street Park on the east side. The children reacted so enthusiastically that the innovation was extended to include both black and white children in several additional parks the following summer.[56]

Progressively throughout the 1880s, city council and the mayor were shorn of their former authority over the apparatus of city government. Wilmington retained merely the shell of a mayor-council system. The council ceased to control appropriations because the commissions habitually asked the state legislature to enact special legislation setting their respective budgets. City council was forced to raise taxes in support of bond sales that they had had no part in approving. The *Every Evening* commented in 1888 that "as a matter of course, council's business has decreased in about the same proportion as its control of the people's money, and the meetings are now as devoid of business as they were formerly overcrowded." There was even talk of dissolving the council altogether.[57]

Halfway to Reform

The commissions gave Wilmington an important boost toward modernization. It is hard to believe that the poorly organized councilmen could ever have produced the parks and utilities that the commissioners made possible. But the creation of commissions left Wilmington with an unintegrated and undemocratic governmental structure. There was no institutional means to umpire conflicts between commissions. In 1894 Mayor Evan Shortlidge, a physician who had served for many years as president of the school board, castigated the commissions as "clumsy, costly, and inefficient. . . . I believe that the people of Wilmington are capable of governing themselves; and I believe that nearly all of our evils and misdirections of government have sprung from the effort so successfully made in recent years to control many of our local affairs by legislation at Dover." While admitting that the commissioners were generally "capable and public-spirited men," he regretted the fact that they had been chosen by the legislature, governor, or a state

[56] *Ibid.*, 1910, p. 19.
[57] *Every Evening*, July 21, 1888.

35. *The Street Cleaning Brigade.* A corps of white-uniformed men called "white wings" were employed to remove manure and trash from the newly paved streets. The center photograph shows #24 School at Fourteenth and Washington streets. *13th Annual Statement of the Board of Directors of the Street and Sewer Department of Wilmington, Delaware* (Wilmington, 1900). (Courtesy H.M.M.L.)

Wilmington, Delaware

judge rather than by the citizens of the city. "I am not ignorant of, nor indifferent to, the ostensible reasons which led many good men in this city eight years ago to deprive Wilmington of local self-government and place the expenditure of our vast sums of money, aggregating millions . . . into the hands of autocratic commissioners," he noted. But now that the crisis had passed, he called for a new system of municipal government that would restore power to the people.[58]

Many of the same people who had supported the commission movement in the 1880s turned their attention to charter reform in the following decade. In 1895 the state legislature appointed a bipartisan committee, consisting of four Wilmington businessmen to consider changes in the city's charter. In February 1897 the committee presented a plan designed to force the political parties to share power and provide clear lines of authority and safeguards against corruption. Under the new charter, city council would become a legislative body with control over the city's budget, and the mayor would become the city's chief executive officer, charged with appointing bipartisan committees to administer the city departments. Only the board of education would continue to be elected directly by the voters.[59] The proposed charter received considerable publicity in the local press and two hundred people, who attended a town meeting to discuss the charter provisions, voted for a resolution in favor of its adoption.[60] Despite this show of enthusiasm, the committee made its report so late in the brief 1897 legislative session that the legislators, who were busy discussing the revision of the state constitution, postponed the Wilmington charter question until 1898.[61]

The committee members and other supporters of charter revision kept the issue before the public.[62] But powerful groups opposed it, including the Pennsylvania Railroad, which disliked a section that would give the city regulatory power over railroads traversing its boundaries, and again in 1898 the legislature adjourned without bringing the measure to a vote.[63] Sponsors

[58] *Every Evening History of Wilmington* (Wilmington, Del., 1894), pp. 80–84.
[59] *Every Evening*, Feb. 26, 1897.
[60] *Ibid.*, Mar. 19, 1897.
[61] *Ibid.*, Mar. 25, 1897.
[62] *Ibid.*, Oct. 20, 1897, Nov. 17, 1897, Feb. 17, 1898.
[63] *Ibid.*, Feb. 17, 1898, Jan. 13, 1899.

66

of the measure, hopeful that a few concessions to special interests might spur passage, dropped the section that had proved objectionable to the railroads. Despite these efforts, the charter bill was again lost. The discouraged committee reported to the board of trade that outright bribery by the charter's enemies had prevented its passage.[64]

x

36. *Market Street in the 1890s*. This photograph looking south from Ninth Street gives impressive evidence of the success of efforts to improve the city's streets and eliminate dirt. Note that trees still grew along the city's principal business street. (Courtesy E.M.H.L.)

to vote.[67] Whichever party controlled each county tax office could exaggerate its following merely by avoiding the acceptance of the taxes of opponents and by paying the taxes of its own supporters among the poor. Addicks, seizing upon this corrupt system, began constructing a viable Republican party in Democrat-leaning Kent and Sussex counties by paying huge numbers of poor citizens, both black and white, to become voters for the first time. The state's Democrats were only a bit more appalled at his tactics than were the respectable lawyers and businessmen who represented the New Castle County G.O.P. Since the regular Republicans refused to support Addicks's ambitions, the party was hopelessly split between the gas king's "Union" Republicans and the regulars. Neither faction could gain sufficient votes to elect a senator, and Delaware had only one representative in the U.S. Senate until 1906, when Colonel Henry du Pont, another wealthy man in politics, built a faction of his own strong enough to defeat Addicks.

Meanwhile, every legislative session was absorbed by the ceaseless political battle while the people of Delaware looked on in helpless fascination. State business was neglected as the politicians made deals and counterdeals to elect a senator. One casualty was the Wilmington charter bill, which itself

[67] Amy M. Hiller, "The Disfranchisement of Delaware Negroes," *Delaware History* 13 (1968): 124.

became a pawn in the senatorial struggle. For in addition to his political ambitions Addicks desired to take control of gas distribution in Wilmington. His ploy in other cities had been to secure a franchise to operate in competition with the established gas company and then to frighten the competitor into selling out to him. His plans were thwarted in Wilmington, however, by the street and sewer commission, which controlled utility franchises. The commission, friendly to the existing Wilmington Gas Company, refused to grant Addicks a franchise. Consequently, Addicks favored charter revision in Wilmington to place control over franchises in a political body, where his Union Republicans might seize control. Addicks's conniving killed hopes for the state legislature to agree on a charter bill.[68]

The failure of Wilmington's civic leaders to win charter reform should not detract from their numerous successes in achieving urban progress. The commissions, though not ultimately the best answer to Wilmington's political needs, transformed the city rapidly and, on the whole, efficiently. A clear measure of the effectiveness of their reforms can be gleaned from the steady drop in Wilmington's death rate from nearly thirty per thousand in the early 1880s to 17.89 in 1893 and 14.64 in 1908.[69] Far from opposing these urban reforms and the increased tax rate that accompanied them, the city's business leaders were in the forefront of the reform movement.

Here is a case where Vera Shlakman's concept of an urban population "balanced" between middle-class and working-class members was a significant factor in the quality of urban life. The lack of social vitality that she portrayed in the factory town of Chicopee, Massachusetts,[70] was mitigated in industrial Wilmington because, unlike Chicopee's industrial magnates, Wilmington's factory owners lived in the city themselves. Gause, Postles, Bancroft, and the other industrial leaders knew that in the long run the continued success of their businesses depended upon the vitality of Wilmington as a whole. With this knowledge, they wrestled with the poorly organized city government, the jealousy of the city council, and the apathy of many of their fellow Wilmingtonians in order to provide the city with public services.

[68] *Every Evening*, Apr. 28, 1897.
[69] *Annual Report of the Board of Health*, 1893–94, 1908.
[70] Shlakman, *Economic History of a Factory Town*, p. 226.

37. *#9 School*, Eighth and Wollaston streets, built in 1895, was a grammar school and the training school for teachers. Photograph ca. 1912. (Courtesy E.M.H.L.)

CHAPTER III

The Formation of an Urban Society, 1840–1870

The study of Wilmington's social progress in the transitional middle years of the nineteenth century must begin with an examination of changes in the city's population. Analysis for this period is limited, however, by the paucity and unreliability of surviving records. Of extant statistics the most significant was the rise in total population from 8,452 to 30,841 in the thirty-year period from 1840 to 1870.[1] The percentage of blacks in the total city population declined somewhat, from 17 percent in 1845 to 10.3 percent by 1870.[2] It is difficult to estimate the increase of foreign-born in the city because the early censuses recorded them in terms of counties rather than small cities, while Wilmington city directories, the other source of population statistics, broke down the population by color only. In 1870 most of Wilmington's foreign-born, who numbered 5,152 or 16.6 percent of the city's people, were Irish.[3]

The first thirty years of the industrial age was a period of rapid transition in the whole socioeconomic pattern of Wilmington's life. The railroad replaced the stagecoach, large factories replaced small units of craftsmen, and industrial craftsmen and office managers replaced the merchants and millers of an earlier day as the community's wealthiest, most powerful men. An increase in the number, diversity, and influence of community associational groups accompanied the acceleration of the economy. Various factors help to explain this social phenomenon. Some increase in the number of churches, fraternal groups, and cultural societies was inevitably the result of the population's growth and greater ethnic diversity. Other factors were the nationwide spirit of reform in the 1830s and 1840s, which emphasized the introduction of public education and other philanthropic endeavors and economic changes that brought new men into positions of prominence. Al-

[1] U.S. Census, 1910, *Population*, 2:268.
[2] *Wilmington City Directory*, 1845; U.S. Census, 1870, *Population and Social Statistics*, 1:97.
[3] U.S. Census, 1870, *Population* . . . , 1:97.

Wilmington,
Delaware

though some students of urban development in this period have argued that reformers in such areas as education and prison reform were inspired by fears of social chaos,[4] Wilmington's major social developments were more closely related to the requirements of the new industrial order. To under stand the phenomenon of community-building in mid-century one must try to recapture the sense of tension that existed between the established professionals and businessmen's fears concerning the possible consequences of unbridled social change and their optimism, not only that they personally were on the threshold of success but that their city and indeed their whole culture was moving swiftly toward material and moral fulfillment. Optimism and the pursuit of order, the two sides of the dynamics of social change, are the keys to understanding Wilmington's institutional development as it progressed from a town governed by inherited tradition to a city characterized by a multitude of public and private organizations.

New Roles for the Churches

The importance of religious institutions as culture carriers in the lives of mid-nineteenth-century Wilmingtonians can hardly be exaggerated. Churches offered not only the most important source of identity and purpose but also opportunities for education, improvement of social position and self-esteem, and rules by which to guide one's life. The identification of peculiar ethnic, class, and attitudinal types with particular denominations and even with specific congregations was taken for granted. By 1840 the Friends had long since ceased to be the most numerous religious group in Wilmington. Presbyterians, Baptists, Episcopalians, Methodists, and Roman Catholics all had established one or more congregations in the town. While these groups would have disagreed on many matters, both theological and social, all shared the fundamental assumption that a good society is an orderly one in which people strive to achieve piety and self-improvement.

At first glance the churches may appear to have represented the essence of conservatism and therefore to have retarded social change. The evidence supports the opposite conclusion, however, that these institutions were in

[4] Rothman, *Discovery of the Asylum,* and Michael B. Katz, *The Irony of Early School Reform: Educational Innovation in Mid-Nineteenth-Century Massachusetts* (Cambridge, 1968).

38. *The Friends' Meeting,* Fourth and West streets. Built in 1817 on a design by Benjamin Ferris the present meetinghouse is the third on the site. (Courtesy H.S.D.)

the forefront of development. In 1814, eighteen years before the first public school was opened in Wilmington, the major denominations inaugurated Sunday schools for the purpose of providing an opportunity for poor children to become literate.[5] In addition to the Quakers, the Methodists and Catholics opened day schools as well. Long before government assumed responsibility for outdoor relief, the Dorcas societies of the various congregations were dispensing charity to needy members and nonmembers alike.[6] The churches pioneered in organized recreation as well, as attested by numerous newspaper items concerning Sunday school steamboat parties to Delaware and New Jersey beaches. And it was the churches, especially the Methodist congregations, that made the first systematic efforts to improve

[5] Montgomery, *Reminiscences*, pp. 119–20.
[6] *Delaware State Journal,* Nov. 20, 1855.

39. *First Presbyterian Church,* the east side of Market Street between Ninth and Tenth streets. The Old Church was removed to Brandywine Park in 1922 to make way for the Wilmington Institute Free Library. The new church was torn down in 1929 when the Delaware Trust Building was constructed on the site. (Courtesy E.M.H.L.)

neighborhood conditions in the east-side slums. It was not by chance that community pride manifested itself in building churches, which were the largest, most elegant edifices in the city.

The progress of Methodism in Wilmington epitomizes the interrelation of a religious body with the total urban society. When Methodist itinerants first preached in Wilmington in the 1760s, their appeal was most strongly felt among the relatively poor and unchurched portion of the population. In 1789 the town's forty-three white and nineteen black converts built a small chapel on Walnut Street named for Bishop Asbury. In spite of attacks on the church by hooligans, the congregation persevered and grew. By 1820 Asbury could count three hundred communicants.[7]

At first the Methodists practiced some degree of racial integration, but after a few years together in the chapel, tensions arose between the races. It was a Methodist practice to hold classes for converts to the faith before they were admitted to full membership. The black converts, who were

[7] Hanna, ed., *Asbury Centennial,* pp. 144–48.

taught separately from the whites, were deeply offended when the membership in 1805 adopted a resolution, "whereas, in consequence of meeting the classes of the Black people on the lower seats of this church, a number of benches have been broken and the house so defiled by dirt, etc., as to render it unfit to meet in. . . . Resolved that no black classes shall hereafter meet on the lower floor of Asbury Church."[8] The incensed black members led by Peter Spencer and William Anderson, black lay preachers, withdrew from Asbury and founded Ezion Church, the first all black society of any kind in Wilmington. Spencer and Anderson and some of their followers were disappointed to discover that the white-dominated conference continued to dictate policy to the new all-black congregation. Their refusal to acknowledge the right of the conference to impose a minister on them led to a civil suit. Seeing that, "if we did not let the church go we might look for nothing but lawing," Spencer and Anderson established a new independent congregation, the African Union Methodist Church, in 1812.[9] It was one of the first black-controlled corporations in the United States and became the mother

[8] *Ibid.*, p. 146.
[9] *The Discipline of the Union American Methodist Episcopal Church,* 1872.

40. *Asbury Methodist Church,* southeast corner Third and Walnut streets. Asbury has had many additions since it was built in 1789. Undated photograph probably from the 1890s. (Courtesy H.S.D.)

church to a conference of black churches throughout the middle-Atlantic region. The African Methodist conference met four times each year. One of these quarterly meetings was traditionally held in Wilmington during August. This meeting, which was designated Big Quarterly, included the celebration of the founding of the conference. Big Quarterly, an event unique to Wilmington, was the principal holiday for black people from the Delmarva peninsula, southern Pennsylvania, and New Jersey. Thousands, both slave and free, descended on French Street wearing their finest apparel to attend services and meet with friends. Bands of spiritual singers and food vendors roamed the street. In pre-Civil War days, crowds estimated as large as 15,000 people participated in the event.[10]

Methodism was the fastest-growing faith in nineteenth-century Wilmington among whites as well as blacks. In 1818 Asbury started a Sunday school that drew many young people from the neighborhood into the church and offered them both an opportunity to learn to read and write and the habit of church attendance. The denomination grew as Wilmington attracted many migrants from southern Delaware where Methodism was the dominant faith. By the 1840s a new generation of Methodists had reached maturity, some of whom became prominent citizens and businessmen in the community. As their social status increased, these men became annoyed with certain practices at Asbury that they regarded as excesses of "primitive Methodism." Unwilling to abandon the denomination in which they had been reared the more successful Methodists decided to found a new Methodist church located nearer their west-side homes. In 1845 this group built St. Paul's Church, which gained a reputation within the Methodist conference as "the silk-stocking church."[11]

The wealthiest members of St. Paul's were also those who were most concerned about the potential for social disorder in the expanding community. Their faith and experience dictated that the church was the institution best suited to condition potentially antisocial individuals to restrained behavior in order to maintain community tranquility. Job Jackson, president of the Jackson & Sharp Car Works, and J. Taylor Gause, president of Harlan & Hollingsworth, led a movement within St. Paul's for the congrega-

[10] Alice Nelson, "Big Quarterly in Wilmington," 1932, typewritten manuscript, W.I.F.L.
[11] Hanna, ed., *Asbury Centennial,* p. 180.

tion to build and staff mission chapels in the city's working-class neighborhoods where, according to a chaplain at one of these missions, "the people were poor, illiterate, and desperately wicked."[12] Jackson and Gause contributed the major portion of funds to found two such neighborhood chapels, and Jackson personally led a half dozen of his coreligionists into the worst east-side area where they sang hymns in the street to attract a few "ragged and dirty urchins" to a newly opened Sunday school in 1863.[13]

In 1860 those most interested in the mission work founded a Sunday school association at St. Paul's to coordinate these efforts. When they proposed to enlarge the church building to provide for more Sunday school rooms, many in the congregation objected and "all the wealthy members,"[14] frustrated by delay, decided to found another new church and to make it the headquarters for their missionary activities.

The building they erected, called Grace Methodist Church, together with the recorded statements about the church by various members is persuasive evidence that Wilmington's Methodist industrial leaders expected organized religion to be a powerful force for community harmony and pride. The church was to be a thank offering to God for a variety of blessings: the progress of Methodism both in Wilmington and throughout the United States, the salvation of the country and of the Philadelphia-Wilmington area in particular as a result of the Union victory at Gettysburg, and the financial rewards of industry, which had made Jackson, Gause, and others among Wilmington's Methodists wealthy men. They decided, therefore, to erect a monumental, fashionable building that would eclipse every other structure in the city and reflect not only the prosperity but the good taste and urbanity of its citizens. The building of Grace Church became almost an obsession with the congregation's leaders. J. T. Gause, writing twenty-five years later, recalled that he and his co-workers were "mysteriously moved by an inspiration they had never experienced before. They felt that they were specially called to share in the responsibilities as well as the successes of the church, and that they were being led along by the Heavenly Father in ways of which they had never dreamed. Indeed, so remarkable

[12] *Ibid.*, p. 219.
[13] *Ibid.*, p. 220.
[14] *Ibid.*, p. 180.

and rich were their blessings that some of them could not even look upon the completed edifice without having their hearts overflow with gratitude in the thought that God had been pleased to use them as His instruments in carrying out His plans and purposes. I firmly believe that the Jews were not more fully under the guidance of Heaven in building the walls of Jerusalem than were we in the building of Grace Church."[15] The building so ecstatically described was a large one (166 feet by 102½ feet) of green-tinted serpentine designed with decorated Gothic motifs, including two towers. It was located at the western edge of the city, within a block of the Delaware Avenue horsecar line, which was being installed simultaneously.[16]

Despite the terrific financial burden of paying for the $200,000 church, the members at Grace proceeded with their plans to make the church a center for citywide Methodist missions. In 1866 they organized the Sunday School Union through which the congregation spent $37,000 over the next quarter century in support of its several mission chapels. Sunday school teachers from Grace went into areas they described as "benighted, belligerant, and uncouth," as if they were going amongst the heathen.[17] A memorial to one such teacher eulogized that through her kindness to the poor who attended the mission "many a home was brightened and many a heart took hope."[18] According to Robert D. Cross, mission churches were at best a mixed blessing in American cities since they were often "colonialist enterprises" blighted by paternalism.[19] It is true that the leaders at Grace and St. Paul's were eager to establish and maintain a system of neighborhood churches in which the congregations representing various socioeconomic levels would remain separate from one another. But there is little evidence in Wilmington to support Cross's statement that mission churches produced

[15] *Proceedings of the 25th Anniversary of the Organization of Grace Methodist Episcopal Church*, 1890, pp. 49–50.
[16] *Wilmington Daily Commercial*, Jan. 23, 1868.
[17] *25th Anniversary of Grace M.E. Church*, pp. 100–1.
[18] *Ibid.*, p. 104.
[19] Robert D. Cross, *The Church and the City* (New York, 1967), p. xvii.

---

41. *Grace Methodist Church Looms Above the City.* Photograph, ca. 1890, taken from the roof of the Law Building, southwest corner Ninth and Market streets, looking west along Ninth Street. (Courtesy H.S.D.)

"feelings of dependence and hostility" for quite a few missions managed to develop sufficient indigenous support to become independent of the mother church. The Wilmington missions served more in the role of parents who relinquished authority once their offspring had reached maturity.

Of all the denominations in nineteenth-century Wilmington, the Methodists were the most important to the city as a whole. Not only did they include among their ranks the greatest number and most varied socioeconomic groups, but their evangelical zeal made a significant impact on the community. While Grace supported missions in poor white neighborhoods, the congregation of Ezion Church undertook a similar ministry among the poor blacks establishing Sunday schools in regions of the city that were described by black Methodist leaders as "notorious for . . . gamblers, drunkards, and low women."[20] A constant problem for the urban missionaries was the peripatetic life-style of most slum residents. Typical of the mission neighborhoods was South Wilmington where workers from Grace reported that the population was "essentially transient, migrating with the tide of commercial prosperity or depression, particularly of the adjacent rolling-mills—one month here and the next gone."[21] Occasionally a mission could attract a core of regular churchgoers and become an independent church,[22] but for the most part the missionaries labored against difficult odds in their efforts to combat lawlessness and ignorance with piety and literacy.

The other Protestant denominations—Presbyterians, Baptists, and Episcopalians—increased their role in social welfare and education only a little less than did the Methodists. Church affiliation was an important means toward establishing respectability in the community. A spectacular demonstration of the role church membership could play in an individual's progress in secular society can be seen in the career of Henry S. McComb who rose from humble beginnings to become Wilmington's wealthiest man in the 1860s. The son of a blacksmith, McComb was orphaned at age seven and apprenticed to a tanner. Although he lacked formal education, he learned to read and write in a Hanover Presbyterian Church school class taught by U.S. District Judge Willard Hall. Hall was so impressed with McComb's talents that he offered the young man a large personal loan by

---

[20] Hanna, *Asbury Centennial,* p. 239.
[21] *25th Anniversary of Grace M.E. Church,* p. 108.
[22] Hanna, *Asbury Centennial,* p. 232.

42. *Saint John's Episcopal Church,* southwest corner Market Street and Concord Avenue. Undated photograph, ca. 1890, includes the Sunday school building. (Courtesy E.M.H.L.)

which McComb was able to go into the tanning business on his own at age eighteen.[23] Without the Hall loan, McComb might have remained a tannery worker. A survey made in the mid-1880s is the only available quantitative data on which to evaluate the impact of these church-sponsored schools on society generally. According to these figures, which are undoubtedly too high, the combined schools of the five churches that reported on their Sunday school membership was 2,745.[24] At that time there were two Quaker meetings, six Presbyterian, ten Methodist, seven Baptist, and four Episcopal churches in the city,[25] each with its own educational program.

While the Protestant churches were in the process of expanding their activities to accommodate what their members saw as the needs of an urban society, the Roman Catholic Church with its tradition of involvement in a wide spectrum of human life, was creating in Wilmington a number of social and educational institutions. A Catholic school and orphanage were established in the city as early as 1830, and in 1839 Father Patrick Reilly, an Irish-born priest, began a boarding school for boys that blossomed into a short-lived collegiate institution.[26] In spite of difficulties in obtaining teaching nuns, the Catholics built parish primary schools in conjunction with each new church they established.[27] A chapter of the Saint Vincent de Paul Society was also founded, which gave aid to Catholics in need similar to the Dorcas societies among the Protestant denominations.

Churches offered an important means by which citizens, particularly among the better-educated and wealthier professional and entrepreneurial groups, could labor on behalf of social peace, but the city's leaders also developed other organizations to further this end. The public school, among the most significant innovations of the first half of the nineteenth century, was one such institution.[28] No other single institution is more representative of the social evolution that accompanied industrialization in Wilmington.

[23] *Every Evening,* Dec. 31, 1881.

[24] Scharf, *History of Delaware,* 2:717–21.

[25] *Ibid.,* pp. 707–25.

[26] Leonard J. Kemski, "A History of Catholicism in Delaware, 1704–1868" (M.A. thesis, University of Delaware, 1965), pp. 63–65.

[27] Mother St. Philip Touhey, "A History of Catholic Education in the Diocese of Wilmington, Delaware" (M.A. thesis, Catholic University of America, 1957), pp. 27–75.

[28] See Michael B. Katz, *The Irony of Early School Reform,* pp. 5–17.

The schools attempted to socialize the mass of middle-class and working-class children to the discipline of working under crowded conditions. Public education also prepared these young people to find places in the economy among the growing ranks of office clerical workers, teachers, or in the truncated version of the old preindustrial apprentice system as it continued to be practiced in large factories.

Expanding Educational Opportunities

Public education was introduced into Wilmington in the 1830s through the efforts of a few determined professional men led by U.S. District Judge Willard Hall, a native of Massachusetts and graduate of that state's common schools and Harvard College. Hall was the author of the 1829 Delaware School Law that provided state aid on a matching basis to those districts that established free schools.[29] Hall, appointed superintendant of public education for New Castle County by the state Legislature, together with a few other professional men, established Public School No. 1 in Wilmington in 1833. The school, which charged a small fee for each student enrolled, was an immediate popular success. By 1836, seven hundred children were crowded into its two rooms, and many others who wished to attend had to be turned away.[30]

During its early years life at Public School No. 1 was rough and tumble. In addition to the problem of overcrowding, the pupils, especially the boys, unaccustomed to the confinement and discipline of the school situation, were obstreperous. A succession of male teachers barely managed to keep order despite the liberal use of the rod. One teacher resorted to carrying a revolver in order to maintain discipline.[31] In the midst of this constant disorder, the teachers attempted to teach the three *R*s plus grammar and the English classics, while in the adjoining room the girls learned needlework in addition to their other basic studies.

[29] Daniel Bates, "Memorial Address on the Life and Character of Willard Hall," *Historical and Biographical Papers*, H.S.D. (Wilmington, Del., 1879), 1:34.
[30] *Sunday Star*, June 24, 1906; Mar. 6, 1908.
[31] Scharf, *History of Delaware*, 2:692.

43. *Judge Willard Hall (1780–1875).* Etching from the
*Biographical and Genealogical History of the State of
Delaware,* 2 vols. (Chambersburg, Pa., 1899), 1:
1899. (Courtesy E.M.H.L.)

As the idea of free public education took hold, many Wilmingtonians came to believe that schooling should be made subject to democratic control, and in 1852 the legislature adopted a new school law that established a popularly elected board of education for the city. Subsequently, therefore, the development of the public school movement in Wilmington was dependent upon widespread public support.[32] The men elected to the new board represented a variety of occupations and points of view. Practical men, including a ship's carpenter, butcher, tailor, and cooper, served on the first board, together with two physicians, several merchants, a private schoolmaster, and Judge Hall, who was chosen president of the body.[33] Hall found the board to be a more effective instrument to improve education than the more remote county committees. Not only did the board build new schools; it also established standards for teachers and conducted a normal school on Saturdays for those who were preparing to take the qualifying test. As children became more acclimated to the school environment, discipline was relaxed somewhat and the board, eager to avoid friction with parents, eliminated the rod.[34] In an effort to keep expenses low while offering a broadened instructional program, the board began replacing male teachers with females who could be had for lower salaries.[35] In 1858 a school examining committee, commenting on the improvements effected by the board during its six-year existence, noted that "instead of about 300 children, miserably accommodated and laboring under many inconveniences, we find 1,800 children almost all well provided for."[36]

Hall continued to press for additional improvements to the school system. From the first, one of his chief arguments in favor of public schools had been that of mobility for those children whose parents could not afford to educate them in private academies.[37] In the late 1850s he appealed to this same reasoning in urging the board of education to open a grammar school.

[32] *Ibid.,* p. 693.
[33] *Delaware State Journal,* July 31, 1855.
[34] *Sunday Star,* Mar. 6, 1898.
[35] According to the *Delaware State Journal,* July 31, 1855, teachers' salaries in the Wilmington public schools ranged from $50.00 to $108.15 per quarter.
[36] *Ibid.,* Jan. 15, 1858.
[37] *Report of the Annual School Convention of New Castle County* (Wilmington, Del., 1849).

Wilmington, Delaware   The board submitted his proposal to a public referendum, where to Hall's acute disappointment the grammar school was defeated. The judge exclaimed that "prejudice has been excited in the minds of some against a grammar school by representing it as a school for the rich, not for the poor." Nothing could be farther from its true value, for the grammar school would in fact be "the school of the industrial classes, to qualify them to be business men . . . with a good grammar school, every man in this city can give his son this education. . . . The greatest hindrance to the education of our youth is in parents not allowing their children to remain at school a proper time."[38] Hall's reasoning may have been naive in that working-class families could not afford to keep their children out of the labor market beyond the primary grades, but the idea of a public grammar school gained popularity among the middle class, and such a school was established less than a decade later without any public debate.

After the Civil War these same arguments for social mobility were rehearsed once more on behalf of a public high school. By this time, partly as a result of the change-over from male to female instructors, teaching was becoming a recognized career objective and normal schools were being organized throughout the country to train young women in the techniques of the profession. Supporters of the high school argued that it would be the capstone of the city's education system, since it would train the teachers who would staff the primary and grammar schools.[39] Simultaneous with the establishment of a public high school in 1871 was the board's closely related decision to appoint a professional superintendent of public education who would assume day-to-day responsibility for the city's fourteen schools while the board relegated itself to the more general aspects of educational policy and financing.

In a recent study devoted to ideological and social factors in the movement for school reforms in nineteenth-century Massachusetts, Michael Katz argues that educational reformers were motivated by fear of social chaos stemming from the urban industrial working class. In Beverly, Massachusetts, a shoemaking town, for example, he found that working-class votes helped to abolish the public high school in 1860. "Contrary to the myth that

[38] *Delaware State Journal,* Mar. 25, 1859.
[39] *Wilmington Daily Commercial,* Apr. 27, 1869.

44. *Wilmington's First Public High School, #1 School.* Located on the east side of French Street between Fifth and Sixth streets, this plain building was designed like the row houses around it. It was built in 1871 and contained the high school department and the office of the superintendent. (Photograph by the author November 1968)

45. *#5 Primary School.* Located on the west side of Walnut Street between Twelfth and Thirteenth streets, #5 was built in 1875 at a cost of $16,885.65 and was described in the *Annual Report of the Board of Education, 1875–76,* as "modern [in] style of architecture, and free from all unnecessary ornamentation." (Photograph by the author April 1969)

views public secondary education as the fulfillment of working-class aspirations, the Beverly vote revealed the social and financial leaders of the town, not the least affluent citizens, as the firmest supporters of the high school," Katz declared.[40]

Wilmington's experience was similar to that of Beverly in that the leaders in the public school movement were themselves well-educated middle-class gentlemen. In 1829 a group of Wilmington artisans founded the Association of Working People of New Castle County to lobby for a variety of reforms, including the abolition of imprisonment for debt, a mechanics lien law, and

[40] Katz, *Irony of Early School Reform,* p. 19.

free public education.[41] Similar workingmen's groups appeared in other American cities at that time to work for these same goals. Most of these organizations, including the Wilmington Association, were short-lived political expressions of artisan anxiety concerning industrialization. The association sponsored a newspaper, the *Delaware Free Press,* whose editor hoped to fill his columns with unsolicited articles and letters about the

[41] Thomas R. Dew, "Delaware's First Labor Party" (M.A. thesis, University of Delaware, 1959), p. 2.

46. *The Willard Hall School.* Built at the northwest corner Eighth and Adams streets in 1889, it served as the high school until 1901. The imposing building, for a time the showpiece of the public school system, reflects a dramatic shift in the public's attitude toward the place of education in just eighteen years after the erection of #1 school. (Courtesy H.S.D.)

47. *The Washington School #24.* Completed in 1894, this school evoked the board of education's building committee to write, "The building cost something more than the plain buildings that have been erected for primary schools. . . . Is it not wise in the erection of public buildings to have some regard to the beauty of the city?" *Annual Report of the Board of Education of the City of Wilmington, 1893–94.* Photograph from George A. Wolf, *Industrial Wilmington* (Wilmington, 1898). (Courtesy E.M.H.L.)

school issue and other concerns of workingmen. Contrary to these expectations, most contributors wrote long theological articles about the Hicksite controversy among the Friends and ignored workingmen's reforms.[42] The experience of the association would suggest that the free public education issue did not excite much comment among Wilmington's artisan class, possibly because Willard Hall was encountering little opposition to his reform legislation.

The board of education, Wilmington's longest-lived and only popularly elected commission, never got so far ahead of public opinion to bring about the kind of acrimonious public debate and class division that occurred in Beverly. Toward the end of the century when the enemies of commission government were campaigning for a new city charter, the reformers agreed that the board of education should be preserved.[43] Over the years the composition of the board shifted away from the professional men of philanthropic intent who had spearheaded the public school movement toward a membership reflecting many social strata in the city. Their greatest power was that of setting the school tax rate for the city which, being good politi-

[42] *Delaware Free Press*, scattered copies, Jan. 1830–Nov. 1832.
[43] *Every Evening*, Feb. 26, 1897.

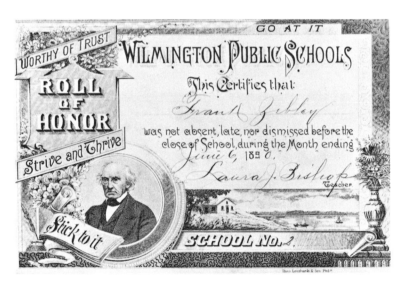

48. *A Good Attendance Award.* This memento of the Wilmington public schools in 1890, complete with a portrait of Judge Hall and moralistic mottoes, suggests something of the attitudes that the schools sought to implant in the young.

cians, they were loath to raise. Consequently, the steady increase in the per capita cost of educating each child from $13.20 per year in 1885–86 to $20.48 in 1900–1901 must be attributed to a gradual shift in public opinion.[44] While teachers' salaries continued to be very low, the board and the community at large took pride in the erection of increasingly pretentious school buildings, which contemporaries believed helped to mark the evolution of Wilmington from a simple town to a handsome city.[45]

[44] *Annual Report of the Board of Education,* 1912, p. 11.

[45] An excellent example of this attitude appears in the board's statement in its 1893–94 *Annual Report* concerning the completion of #24 School on Washington Street, a castellated brick edifice with copper trim: "The building cost something more than the plain buildings that have been erected for primary schools. . . . Is it not wise in the erection of public buildings to have some regard to the beauty of the city?"

Table 2. Growth of the school system by 5-year intervals

Year	Number of schools	Enrollment	Number of teachers
1873	15	5,920	82
1878	18	6,831	110
1882	19	7,123	117
1887	24	8,814	167
1892	27	9,463	193
1897	28	10,749	226

SOURCE: *Board of Education Annual Report,* 1896–97, p. 14.

Table 3. School attendance in 1910

	Number in school	% of total in school
Native-born whites, 6–9 years old	2,419	75.5%
Negroes " " "	419	72.6%
Foreign-born whites " " "	153	65.9%
Native-born whites, 15–20 years old	1,578	29.0%
Negroes " " "	241	25.0%
Foreign-born whites " " "	41	3.9%

SOURCE: Federal Census, *Population,* 1:1167.

Table 4. Cost of schools per child attending

Year	Amount
1885–86	$13.20
1890–91	16.61
1895–96	17.68
1900–01	20.48
1905–06	25.72
1910–11	26.00

SOURCE: *Board of Education Annual Report,* 1896–97, p. 12; *Board of Education Annual Report,* 1912, p. 11.

Table 5. Size of high school graduating classes

Year	Number of boys	Number of girls
1875	11	10
1880	13	16
1885	16	24
1890	27	23
1894	27	36

SOURCE: *Board of Education Annual Report,* 1896–97, p. 18.

David W. Harlan, the man who served as superintendent from 1871 until his death in 1900, was an experienced teacher whose modesty and sensitivity to the attitudes of an industrial community were in harmony with the majority of the board members' views. Harlan organized the schools into a completely unified system. He established a one-year normal school program beyond high school for those seeking appointments in the public schools. He was an eager advocate of "object teaching," a technique popular among late-nineteenth-century educators designed to challenge children's interest, and he urged teachers to rely upon "skill and tact" rather than force in dealing with their pupils.[46] Harlan carefully refrained from joining the

[46] *First Annual Report of the Board of Education,* 1872, p. 1.

on-going public debate during the 1870s and 1880s concerning the purpose of the high school. Some believed that the high school was primarily a free academy that should aim at giving its students a classical education in preparation for college. Others, who emphasized the democratic nature of a public school, said that it should prepare young men for apprenticeships and clerical work.[47] Harlan was eventually dragged into the argument when a newspaper reporter questioned him about the classics issue. His response was in line with the latter position—that Latin was out of place in a public school because the taxpayers were being asked to underwrite a course of instruction relevant only to a few students from wealthy families.[48]

Harlan attempted to meet the needs of working-class youngsters. As early as 1873 he urged the adoption of a compulsory school law, noting that "the frequent appearance of youthful offenders before our courts shows how this class of children is being educated."[49] Such a law was not passed in Delaware until 1911 because of powerful opposition from rural areas.[50] He recognized the relationship between truancy and corporal punishment and told the teachers that school should be made as pleasant as possible since "there is a growing conviction that even very bad children ought to be governed by something higher and better than the rod."[51] But, other than maintaining a night school, he found no adequate means by which the schools could serve working boys and girls.

During its first thirty years, the high school did serve a limited clientele. In the mid-1870s only one-fifth of those completing the primary grades went on to the grammar school; the percentage went up only a little to one-fourth over the next twenty years.[52] If grammar school attendance was low, that of the high school was lower still. The first graduating class of the high school in 1875 consisted of only eleven boys and ten girls. Generally speaking, females outnumbered males in late-nineteenth-century graduating classes, a reflection of the close relationship between high school graduation and the

---

[47] *Every Evening*, Sept. 23, 1873; July 18, 1883.
[48] *Ibid.*, July 19, 1883.
[49] *Annual Report of the Board of Education*, 1874–75, p. 3.
[50] *Annual Report of the Board of Education*, 1911, p. 51.
[51] *Annual Report of the Board of Education*, 1872–73, p. 39.
[52] *Annual Report of the Board of Education*, 1874–75, p. 7; 1896–97, p. 9.

teaching profession. In 1885 the number rose to sixteen boys and twenty-four girls, while in 1894 twenty-seven boys and sixty-two girls graduated.[53] Male graduates followed a much wider variety of career patterns, according to a listing of all graduates for the school's first two decades made by the Wilmington High School Alumni Association in 1895. The most common jobs for male graduates were those of clerk-bookkeepers (50), draftsmen (13), lawyers (12), physicians (11), engineers (9), and male stenographers (7).[54]

These figures on high school attendance and their relationship to career choice demonstrate the decided orientation toward industrial labor in Wilmington's employment pattern during that period. The main beneficiaries of the high school were the sons and daughters of shopkeepers, white-collar clerical workers and some skilled workers who could not or would not have sent their children to private schools, but who could afford to withhold them from the work force during their adolescence. Those who were most in the high school's debt were the scores of young women who used their high school training as a steppingstone to careers in public education. Although it was a poorly paid profession, teaching carried more prestige, demanded a greater personal commitment, and provided more satisfaction than employment in domestic, factory, and clerical jobs, the only other occupations open to women.

The rise of the public high school coincided with changes in the structure of many of Wilmington's leading businesses. Whereas the first generation of industrial executives came out of the ranks of skilled workmen and had been educated through apprenticeships, the men of the second generation were more likely to have been educated in school. Both Samuel Harlan and Elijah Hollingsworth were the products of apprenticeships, but their successor to leadership in the company they headed was J. T. Gause whose background included academy training and office work.[55] George Lobdell, another apprentice-trained company owner, sent his nephew to college to

---

[53] *Annual Report of the Board of Education*, 1896–97, p. 14.

[54] The Executive Committee of the Alumni, *Biographical Catalogue of the Graduates of the Wilmington High School, 1875–1895* (Wilmington, Del., 1895).

[55] McCarter and Jackson, *Historical and Biographical Encyclopaedia of Delaware*, p. 569.

Wilmington, study engineering.[56] Job Jackson's heir was a high school and college gradu-
Delaware ate. Although the paucity of statistical information makes it impossible to
isolate the high school as a specific factor in the interrelationship between a
changing job market and mobility in Wilmington, the social distance between skilled workers and industrial executives increased as the popularity
of formal schooling grew among the middle class.

The separate development of public schools for blacks is an example of
the pattern, previously noted in regard to religion, of black institutions par-
alleling those of the whites in the nineteenth century city. Unlike the case of
their churches, however, black Wilmingtonians had little or no control over
the schools their children attended. The school law of 1829 excluded blacks
from payment of the school tax and thus made them ineligible to participate
in school board elections until the law was changed in 1905.[57]

Emancipation supplied the impetus for a campaign to include blacks
in the public school system. Most of Wilmington's industrial leaders were
members of the Republican Party, and while as a group they did not favor
racial equality, some of them took seriously the task of helping the newly
enfranchised blacks to become responsible, self-supporting citizens. Education seemed to offer the most direct means to this end. It was in this spirit
of paternalistic uplift that a group of Wilmington civic leaders—including
U.S. District Judge Willard Hall, Episcopal Bishop Alfred Lee, both natives
of New England, and a number of businessmen, mostly Quakers—founded
the Delaware Association for the Moral Improvement and Education of the
Colored People of the State in 1866. Modeled on a similar organization in
Maryland, the association solicited funds to build and maintain primary
schools for black adults and children throughout the state. Although some
blacks attended association meetings, none were elected to leadership positions, and as a group they played a passive role in the life of the organization.

Something of the spirit in which the members undertook their self-

[56] Interview conducted by John Scafidi and Faith Pizor with W. Stewart Allmond, June 10
and July 1, 1969, transcription, E.M.H.L.
[57] Lyman P. Powell, *The History of Education in Delaware* (Washington, D.C., 1893), p.
169; *Annual Report of the Board of Education,* 1905–6, p. 5.

appointed task of educating the state's blacks is revealed in statements in the first annual report:

> We admit, at the outset, the extremely low physical, mental and even moral condition to which years of systematic oppression and degradation have, in many instances, reduced these poor people. . . . Yet such considerations are far from impairing our confidence, or relieving our convictions, in regard to the propriety, nay the absolute duty, of resolutely undertaking the cause of the oppressed and degraded. . . . We hope and believe that well conducted schools will do much to improve the morals as well as inform the minds of a long depressed class, that their influence will be eminently favorably to sobriety, integrity, industry, and Christian principles.[58]

The association had already established several day schools and a night school in Wilmington before the city council agreed to contribute $5,000 toward the erection of a permanent schoolhouse for blacks named for General O. O. Howard, director of the Federal Freedman's Bureau, which supplied the bulk of the building fund. The association administered the school for several years before the city school board agreed to assume responsibility for the black school, and the role of the association in Wilmington education ended.[59] The school board's attitude toward its black schools was conditioned by partisan politics. Generally speaking, Republicans accepted at its word the federal government's demand that blacks be treated equally, and therefore Republicans argued that the city must maintain separate but equal facilities lest the federal courts intervene to establish a single, integrated school system. Democrats, however, doubting both the power and sincerity of the federal government, sought to evade all responsibility for black education while claiming that the Republicans were seeking integration.[60] The school board initially accepted the Howard School into the public system when there was a Republican majority on the board. In the years that followed, Democratic board members were reluctant to im-

---

[58] Minute Book of the Delaware Association for the Moral Improvement and Education of the Colored People, H.S.D.

[59] *Wilmington Daily Commercial*, Jan. 7, 1870; Mar. 12, 1870.

[60] *Ibid.*, Oct. 10, 1871.

prove the Howard School whereas at least a few among the Republicans in-sisted that the black schools be kept up to the standard of the white schools.[61]

The condition of the black schools mirrored the role of blacks generally in the community. Because they were ineligible to vote in school board elections, blacks could bring no political force to bear on the body that controlled decision-making for the schools. The board moved slowly to bring the black schools up to the standards of the other public schools. For example, the Howard School had no high school department to train potential teachers until 1891, twenty years after the all-white Wilmington High School had been established. Since many of Wilmington's blacks drifted from job to job and place to place, their children often failed to establish a routine of going to school. Black youngsters had a higher truancy and with-drawal rate than whites.[62]

Formal education was unrelated to vocational opportunities for most black youths since they could not aspire to any job except that of an un-skilled laborer. Not surprisingly, most of the graduates in the early classes at Howard High School were girls who entered the corps of public school teachers. Ironically, Wilmington's segregated school system offered many more teaching positions to blacks than did the integrated schools of cities to the north. But formal schooling had little relevance for most black males, who were doomed to lives as unskilled workers. In the 1890s, in an effort to keep young men in school, manual training was introduced at Wilmington High School and at Howard, but the principal of the black school reported that "our boys cannot gain admission as apprentice boys to the shops of the city, therefore it would seem like wasted time for them to take up iron

---

[61] *Every Evening,* Dec. 24, 1878.

[62] *Annual Report of the Board of Education,* 1876–77, p. 25; 54 percent of those enrolled in the city's two largest schools for blacks at the beginning of 1876 withdrew before the end of the year. School attendance was considerably lower among black students compared with native whites. In 1890 when 56.5 percent of the native white youngsters between the ages of five and nine were in school, only 43 percent of the black children in that age group were enrolled. Among the ten- to fourteen-year-olds, the difference was greater still: 42.5 percent blacks in school compared to 85.8 percent whites. In the fifteen to nineteen group 11.5 percent of the blacks were in school compared to 21.2 percent of the whites. U.S. Census, 1890, *Population,* 2:134, 172, 174, 180.

49. *Edwina Kruse, Principal of the
Howard School (1876–1921).*
(Courtesy of the Woods Haven–
Kruse School, Delaware State De-
partment of Health and Social
Services)

work, but a good course in upholstering would give them a trade with which
they could earn a living."[63]

From its beginnings in the days of the Delaware Association during Re-
construction, black education was not oriented toward preparing young
people to meet economic challenges but to be acculturated into a white-
controlled world. Morals, Christian training, and good citizenship were the
hallmarks of the association's educational effort. Once blacks had mas-
tered these values, the association's leaders believed that white prejudice
would have no further foundation in fact and true equality would somehow
emerge. Clearly in an economic system that systematically relegated the
overwhelming majority of blacks to the lowest, least skilled jobs, such a no-
tion was illusory. Yet so-called friends of the Negro and the tiny black middle class could see no alternative to continuing to regard education as the
ladder to a better future, and for a few blacks such as schoolteachers, minis-
ters, and a handful of other professionals, it was. The chief difference between white and black education was not so much content or even frame of

[63] *Annual Report of the Board of Education*, 1905.

reference (the nineteenth-century white schools were just as concerned with instilling morality and responsibility as the black schools), but rather the way educational developments paralleled shifts in the economy. In the white community, rising prosperity and the expansion of office jobs as clerks, salesmen, and the like went hand in hand with the rise of the high school. The black community could not participate in this fundamental economic change. Hence at the end of the period, ca. 1910, the black's economic world still had a preindustrial caste to it with many unskilled workers and a few trained professionals. Regardless of the fact that the Howard School offered the same courses as Wilmington High, the social significance of these two schools was far apart—the former represented the aspirations of a race, the latter fulfillment.

The development of public education for white students demonstrated the rapidity with which society adjusted to the tremendous social forces for change inherent in industrialization and urbanization. The public school system not only reflected the indigenous cultural and vocational aims of the city's people, but the schools also drew young people together from differing backgrounds into a common, shared experience. The school transferred the child from a family setting to an impersonal, crowded, regimented environment remarkably similar to that of a factory or large office. Education reflected life.

Social Life and Self-Improvement

The new organizational modes that were affecting the city's response to industrialization extended beyond religion and formal education to encompass such other social activities as debating societies, library companies, and lodges. As with the schools and churches, the development and strengthening of these societies coincided with industrialization. The success of the lodges and self-improvement organizations can be attributed both to the needs of people in an industrializing society and growing city for new sources of social contacts and to the shifting balance among Wilmington's social classes. The latter provided the community with a substantial group of professional men and manufacturer-executives, who took the lead in creating and sustaining these social and cultural organizations although they were by no means the only citizens to profit from them.

The beginnings of self-improvement educational societies in Wilmington predated the town's growth into an industrial center, but these organizations grew considerably during the early stages of industrialization in the late 1830s and 1840s. In those years when most of Wilmington's successful manufactories were getting under way, many young men in the community had reason to be optimistic about their own potential roles in the city's development. Some whose book learning was meager were rising to prominence as officers in manufacturing companies and their eagerness to achieve respect and a wider knowledge of the world was a primary impetus to the growth of self-improvement societies. These societies, with names such as the Young Men's Library and Debating Society, the Franklin Lyceum, and the Young Men's Association for Mutual Improvement, had vague, high-flown ambitions for scholarly endeavor and education. They acquired reading rooms that subscribed to the latest books and periodicals, and some bought scientific equipment for experiments and demonstrations. By the 1850s it was clear to their members that one large association combining the funds and libraries of all would be far superior to their precarious individual existences. Joshua T. Heald, president of the Young Men's Association, convinced the others to merge into the Wilmington Institute.[64]

The history of the institute demonstrated that by the 1860s Wilmington society had achieved a healthy measure of cultural and social integration, for the organization attracted members from every walk of life. In 1860 the institute's sixty charter members, mostly professional men and manufactory executives who had been active in the earlier debating societies, decided to build a large hall containing a library and a lecture room with a seating capacity for eight hundred. They hoped thereby to "encourage a taste for reading and mental culture in a community," which they acknowledged to be "closely occupied with industrial pursuits." They sought especially to meet the needs of those young factory operatives who lived in boardinghouses or amid depressing home environments and were easily enticed away from self-improvement into "drinking rooms and gambling saloons."[65] Toward this end the institute emphasized practical scientific subjects rather than literature and the arts in its lecture series and book pur-

[64] *A Historical Sketch of the Wilmington Library and Young Men's Association* (Wilmington, Del., 1858), pp. 11–12.
[65] *Annual Report of the Wilmington Institute*, 1862, p. 21.

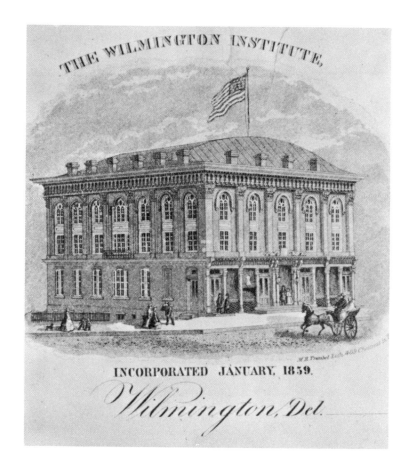

50. *The Wilmington Institute.* Built in 1861, northwest corner Fifth and Market streets. Lithograph by M. H. Traubel of Philadelphia. (Courtesy H.S.D.)

chases. Their appeal to workingmen met with considerable initial success as revealed by a list of the entire membership of 560 people published in 1868. The occupations of 280 of the total are given in the city directory for that year. Of this number 31 were professional men, a similar number were owners or officers in manufacturing firms, 41 were retail merchants, 35 clerks, and 60, by far the largest category, were listed as skilled and semi-skilled workmen.[66]

[66] *Ibid.*, 1868, pp. 26–32.

51. *The Wilmington Institute.* Undated photograph. (Courtesy W.I.F.L.)

52. *Students Preparing for Business Careers at the Wilmington Commercial College.* Photograph from the *Every Evening History of Wilmington* (Wilmington, 1894). (Courtesy E.M.H.L.)

Throughout its life as a private agency from 1859 to 1894, the leadership of the institute continued to be business and professional men. Their continuing concern to make the institute's collections and lectures relevant to a broad public, particularly among the city's many industrial workmen, should not be dismissed as cynical paternalism designed to keep the working class docile and content. Rather, it reflected the belief reinforced by the course of many of their own careers that a highly motivated individual could rise above poverty and lack of education if the means to self-improvement were made available to him. Their commitment was to a style of culture that was indigenous to an industrial community rather than to something false and imposed from above. That the institute served the needs of various economic groups can best be seen in its mechanical drawing school. The institute began offering night classes in mechanical drawing in the 1880s as a means of supplementing the practical training that apprentices received at major industrial firms. The classes took some of the burden of training off the companies, but it was also convenient for apprentices and anyone else who wished to learn drawing, especially since the large companies underwrote part of the expenses. These classes attracted large numbers of students. In 1886 alone, 126 signed up for the course.[67] In addition to the training the school provided, it also served as an unofficial employment bureau for its graduates.[68]

The evidence of Wilmington's course of development suggests that urbanization and industrialization did not necessarily produce a split between entrepreneurs and workingmen that left the latter with sharply reduced cultural and social opportunities and fragmented the community. Although the segregation of neighborhoods on the basis of wealth did occur, the resilience that people in all social classes demonstrated in forging social and cultural patterns relevant to the new economy gave the community considerable integrity and structure. In addition to the evolution of the roles of the churches, schools, and of a cultural association such as the institute, the people of the mid-nineteenth century created two other important kinds of enterprises—the daily newspaper and the fraternal organization that helped to overcome problems of individual or family isolation.

The introduction of inexpensive daily newspapers to Wilmington in the

[67] *Ibid.*, 1887, p. 15.
[68] *Ibid.*, 1890, p. 16.

CLAYTON HOUSE.

53. *The Clayton House, Wilmington's First Hotel,* was built in 1873, on the northeast corner of Fifth and Market streets at the instigation of the board of trade. The hotel was heated by steam and contained 105 rooms, plus public rooms on the ground floor. (Courtesy E.M.H.L.)

1860s was a major step toward imparting information, excitement, entertainment, and a sense of participation in the community to many people.
Prior to the rise of the dailies, Wilmington was served by various weekly
newspapers, for the most part highly partisan, that concentrated on publishing national and world news since local events were passed by word of
mouth more quickly than they could be recorded by a weekly. Wilmington's
proximity to Philadelphia and Baltimore may have retarded her journalism
for it was not until 1866 that a successful daily, the *Wilmington Daily Commercial,* was launched in the city. The two-cent paper was Republican in
politics and made its appeal to the businessmen of the city. The *Commercial's* exclusivity led eventually to its downfall in 1877 when the paper was
bought out by its chief rival, the *Every Evening.* Founded in 1871 by William T. Croasdale, a native of New Castle County and experienced newspaper editor, the *Every Evening,* a penny paper, became the city's chief
newspaper. Croasdale aimed at a mass market; he promised that his paper
would be "a vehicle for news rather than an organ for opinion" and pledged
that "we shall permit the entrance of nothing into our columns unfit to be
read aloud by the father of a family in the presence of his wife and children."[69] The entrance of the *Every Evening* was well timed, its editor
capable and vigorous. Although Croasdale leaned toward Democratic politics, his paper retained its integrity by staying aloof from factions. The
Every Evening concentrated upon local news and backed crusades for public improvements and for more cultural activities in the city. In 1882 Croasdale left the *Every Evening* for a brief stint with the Baltimore *Gazette* before joining Henry George's single-tax crusade as editor of the *New York
Standard,* the George organ.[70] In the 1880s several other dailies were begun
in Wilmington, principally the Republican *Morning News* and an independent Sunday paper, the *Star.*[71] These papers followed the *Every Evening*
formula of presenting themselves as high-minded friends of community
improvements and reform. The establishment of newspapers representing
more than one position on partisan issues made for a political climate in

[69] *Every Evening,* Sept. 4, 1871.
[70] *Ibid.,* Aug. 10, 1891.
[71] Henry C. Conrad, *History of the State of Delaware,* 3 vols. (Wilmington, Del., 1908),
3:1101–4.

54. *Cigar Store Patrons.* In *This Was Wilmington* (Wilmington, 1945), p. 51, newspaperman A.O.H. Grier recalled the "cigar store senates" of the 1880s and 1890s, who gathered regularly at their favorite cigar store to discuss politics and business. Photograph taken in 1890 at Tenth and Market streets. (Courtesy E.M.H.L.)

which the politicians had to be more wary of public opinion while the citizenry was kept better informed about local government issues than at any time in the past.

While the newspapers were helping to knit the growing city together as a viable community, people turned to smaller organizations to give them a sense of personal involvement and security in the impersonal world around them. For some the church fulfilled this role, but many people, especially men, sought out additional opportunities for social contacts by joining fraternal organizations. Lodges enjoyed phenomenal growth during the middle years of the century as men swarmed to join each new order as it was introduced into the city. The Masons, who established a lodge in Wilmington in 1769, were first in the field.[72] By the 1880s there were ten Masonic lodges in the city. In 1831 a second order, the Odd Fellows, was established. By 1883 they claimed twenty-five hundred members in Wilmington, divided into ten lodges. In the course of the 1850s, the Red Men became popular, while a decade later the Knights of Pythias founded six lodges in one year alone. By 1880 Wilmington was supporting twenty-seven lodges, each with a membership of two hundred or more.[73] Since many men joined more than one order, it is impossible to estimate the total number of Wilmington males who belonged to at least one such organization. In addition to the whites-only lodges, there were two black ones—the Hiram Grand Lodge of the Masonic Order and the Star of Bethlehem Lodge of the Odd Fellows,[74] another indication of the practice common among Wilmington's nineteenth-century black population to adopt organizational forms similar to those of white society.

Fraternal organizations attracted professional men, businessmen, and skilled workers. Although the lodges were primarily social outlets that gave people the opportunity to meet together that the industrial economy denied them, they also provided practical assistance to families in need. The years of their greatest popularity coincided with the time when society was in a transitional period. The extended family was declining as an economic and social unit, and modern commercial insurance and labor unions had not yet arisen. The death and sickness benefits that commonly accom-

[72] *Ibid.*, 2:440.
[73] *Ibid.*, pp. 440–48.
[74] *Wilmington Daily Commercial*, June 19, 1867; June 25, 1867.

panied lodge membership were strong inducements to join at a time when there was neither workmen's compensation nor unemployment pay. Furthermore, lodge membership ensured the attendance of many mourners at a deceased member's funeral, an important consideration among nineteenth-century Americans. One example will suffice to show the significance of these security provisions. In 1903 when the Friendly Order of Eagles established its first lodge in Wilmington, it quickly attracted hundreds of working-class people to its rolls.[75] The F.O.E.'s success was largely the result of its extensive benefit program that included free doctors' calls for members and their families, daily payments during sickness, and the payment of funeral expenses.[76]

Ethnic associations constituted another set of voluntary organizations in Wilmington. Although Wilmington attracted relatively fewer immigrants than did many American industrial cities,[77] natives of Ireland and Germany were sufficiently numerous to support a variety of beneficent, athletic, and other social groups, most of which had their headquarters at the Irish Hall or the German Hall, both located near Sixth and French streets. Germans maintained the only local foreign-language newspaper, the *Freie Presse,* owned the city's three breweries, and managed many saloons.[78] Their various societies, including the *Turnverein* and *Sängerbund,* sponsored an annual *Volksfest* that drew large crowds.

The appearance and growth of churches, schools, newspapers, and fraternities demonstrates Wilmingtonians' rapid adjustment to the displacements caused by industrialization and urbanization. Had the owners of Wilmington's industries lived somewhere else, as was the case[79] in many New England mill towns, it is unlikely that the city could have made the adjustment so easily, for the industrial leaders were frequently in the forefront among the initiators of these new social forms. But just as important was the response of those many skilled and clerical workers who were quick

[75] *Sunday Star,* June 21, 1903.

[76] *Ibid.*

[77] Foreign-born constituted 16 percent of Wilmington's total population in 1870. U.S. Census, 1870, *Population and Social Statistics,* 1:97.

[78] J. Emil Abeles, "The German Element in Wilmington from 1850 to 1914" (M.A. thesis, University of Delaware, 1948), p. 32.

[79] Shlakman, *Economic History of a Factory Town,* pp. 24–47.

to seize opportunities to participate in the social order that was in the process of formation. The dynamic trend toward cultural and social integration in the city counterbalanced the forces of isolation and conflict.

55. *View of Wilmington's East Side.* Photograph taken from the roof of the Ford Building on the southwest corner of Tenth and Market streets, ca. 1900. Old and new First Presbyterian churches are in the foreground separated by a burial ground. The large building with the flat roof in the center of the photograph is the McLear & Kendall carriage factory built in 1864 on the southeast corner of Ninth and King streets. The spire in the left center is that of Ezion Methodist Church. Just behind it is the Franklin Cotton Mill. At the center of the photograph toward the rear is St. Mary's R. C. Church. (Courtesy H.S.D.)

110

CHAPTER IV

Industrial Wilmington Comes of Age

In the last thirty years of the nineteenth century, Wilmington reached maturity as an industrial city. Although the population more than doubled from 30,000 in 1870 to 76,000 by 1900, the patterns of land use, occupations, and sources of community leadership established in mid-century persisted. Trends that had begun in the previous decades culminated in a social order that by the 1890s was more institutionalized and more varied than ever before. By the turn of the century, the city achieved its fullest development, both as a center for heavy industry and as a socially integrated environment.

One important element in Wilmington's course of growth during this period was the continued residence of wealthy and middle-class families in the city rather than in unattached suburbs. This phenomenon can largely be explained by the city's relatively small size and slow but steady rate of growth. In late nineteenth-century America mass transit, usually in the form of the trolley car, played a decisive role in shaping urban development.[1] In Wilmington, where there was less potential for great profits in the traction industry, expansion was gradual and conservative.[2]

By the late 1880s population had outstripped the existing housing and transportation facilities, and land developers began building speculative houses immediately to the north and west of the settled regions of the city. Pressures from these real estate promoters induced the Wilmington City Railway Company to electrify and to extend its service into these developing regions. It was not until the turn of the century, however, when the traction company faced competition from a more aggressive rival, the Peoples Railway Company, that trolley lines were extended beyond the city

[1] See, for example, Sam B. Warner, *Streetcar Suburbs: The Process of Growth in Boston, 1870–1900* (Cambridge, Mass., 1962).

[2] *Every Evening*, Apr. 14, 1882; Nov. 9, 1886; Aug. 25, 1887.

limits.[3] Only then did noncontiguous "streetcar suburbs" appear around Wilmington.

The dynamics of Wilmington's growth that kept the various social classes within the city did not, of course, obscure social lines, but it did militate against the upper and middle classes' becoming apathetic about the city as a whole. The attitudes that motivated Wilmington's industrial and commercial leaders are best reflected in Henry Seidel Canby's nostalgic but analytical memoir of his childhood in Wilmington during the 1890s, entitled *The Age of Confidence*.[4] Canby, the son of a Quaker foundry executive, was fascinated, in retrospect, by the character and values of Wilmington's business elite, their application to work, their exclusivity, their insistence on unostentatious comfort, and their lack of intellectual sophistication.

"Our society in the town was thus a class society," Canby concluded. "There were the Negroes, and the working people, and the 'plain people,' and Us. . . ." The classes that appeared to be so exclusive were in fact overlapping and volatile. "As for the 'plain people,'" he wrote, "they were the pit from which we were dug. Most of Us had relatives among them. . . . The difference between them and Us was a subtle one of manners and tradition, chiefly tradition, for our manners were not always good. . . . The families in our absurdly self-conscious upper class were often stuffy people whose intellectual life was bounded by a set of Dickens and a steel print of the Stag at Eve; yet there was a security in their houses that was more than ordinary manners. We stuck by our class, which, in its small town exclusiveness, put up stiffer barriers than the societies of New York or Philadelphia which we supposed to be just like our own, except more promiscuous and more extravagant."[5] The "plain people," Canby explained, were the middle class, people who lived without reference to the past and therefore, from Canby's point of view, lacked the dignity necessary to be included among "Us."

In word pictures Canby recalled how the physical configurations of the city mirrored its class structure. "From the ballroom at the top of the Opera

[3] C. A. Weslager, *Brandywine Springs, Rise and Fall of a Delaware Resort* (Wilmington, Del., 1949), pp. 69–83.

[4] Henry Seidel Canby, *The Age of Confidence* (New York, 1934), pp. 17–19.

[5] *Ibid.*, pp. 19, 20.

112

House where we went for dancing school there was a view of the whole town at once. . . . The factory districts below were grimy and bare, but to the north and west the roofs were hid in a forest with only a 'mansion' here and there or a church steeple projecting. . . . To the southward of the hill-tops lived the 'plain people' by thousands in rows of brick houses with identical windows and doors . . . and below them again, reaching down into the factories were the slums, where congestion was painful, dirty water ran over broken pavements, and the yards behind were reduced to a dump heap. . . . Each neighborhood outside the slums was a little town in itself, with a store or two, a livery stable, wooden houses tucked in behind for the darkies, vacant lots held for speculation, solid dwellings of quality,

56. *Mansions of the 1870s*, 1400 and 1401 Delaware Avenue. 1400 was the home of Washington Jones, president of a Morocco company; 1401 belonged to John H. Adams, a foundry executive. (Courtesy H.S.D.)

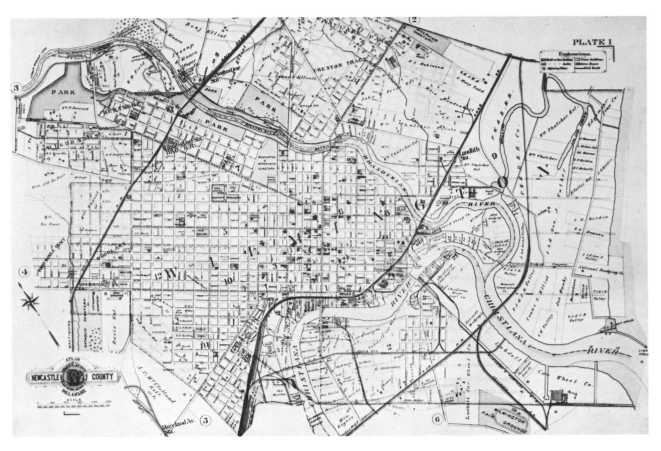

Map 6. *Baist's Atlas, New Castle County* (Philadelphia: G. W. Baist, 1893), plate 1, shows the expansion of the city north of the Brandywine and west of Union Street. (Courtesy E.M.H.L.)

raw built mansions of the new rich, and rows of little houses for the 'plain people.' "[6]

This firsthand description of Wilmington in the 1890s shows that the city was highly stratified and consequently not immune to class and ethnic antagonisms. It may, therefore, seem surprising that the last thirty years of the nineteenth century in Wilmington were so tranquil. In that period the city suffered only one brief race riot, unmarked by fatalities, and sustained only one lengthy but peaceful strike. Although it is generally easier to hypothesize about the causes of dissention rather than those of tranquility, there are four major factors which explain the peace in this industrial city. Briefly stated these factors are: (1) the make-up of Wilmington's population, (2) the nature of the city's industries, (3) the expression of *noblesse oblige* among the families of the business elite, and (4) the flowering of organized, often professional, sports and amusements. This chapter will explore each of these factors.

The Composition of the Population

Labor historians have found that worker militancy was greatly influenced by the ethnic make-up of various industrial cities.[7] Compared to most other east-coast industrial cities, Wilmington's population included a low percentage of immigrants. In 1860 for example, 18.86 percent of Wilmingtonians were foreign-born compared to 28.93 percent in Philadelphia, and 24.71 percent in Baltimore. Of the twenty-seven American cities with populations between 20,000 and 50,000, Wilmington ranked fourth-lowest in its percentage of foreign-born.[8] This pattern persisted. In 1880, 86.6 percent of Wilmington's 42,478 people were native-born Americans; 24,677 of them were born in Delaware, 5,759 in Pennsylvania, and 3,677 in Maryland.[9]

[6] *Ibid.,* pp. 8–10.
[7] See, for example, Patrick Renshaw, *The Wobblies* (Garden City, N.Y., 1967), Chapter 5, entitled "Lawrence and Paterson," and Donald B. Cole, *Immigrant City* (Chapel Hill, N.C., 1963).
[8] U.S. Census, *Population,* 1860, 1:xxxii.
[9] *Ibid.,* 1880, p. 536.

Again in 1900 the census showed that only 13.6 percent of Wilmingtonians were foreign-born.[10]

Most of the foreigners who settled in Wilmington came from groups that had relatively few assimilation problems. In 1880, for example, 3,644 of the city's 5,674 foreign-born were Irish, 768 Germans, and 903 British, while the remainder were from other western European countries. Many of these people were skilled workers. According to the 1900 census, 53.2 percent of Wilmington's foreign-born males were employed in skilled and semiskilled industrial jobs; only 24 percent were unspecified laborers.[11]

Table 6. Ethnic composition of the population by wards

	1890			1910		
Ward	Native white	Foreign white	Negro	Native white	Foreign white	Negro
1	1,910	552	324	1,619	597	428
2	3,456	1,011	773	3,030	1,413	757
3	3,921	919	313	3,961	1,201	277
4	2,979	713	338	2,741	632	443
5	5,429	689	1,290	7,250	1,571	1,202
6	3,758	414	1,184	3,448	370	2,218
7	6,593	989	1,069	12,174	1,551	1,249
8	6,109	997	1,138	6,761	1,027	1,221
9	3,190	782	652	8,731	1,221	647
10	4,082	934	—	5,588	1,007	58
11	1,738	658	102	4,401	2,365	45
12	1,540	391	494	4,927	723	536

SOURCE: U.S. Census, 1890, *Population,* 1:526; 1910, *Population,* 2:283.

Anti-Catholicism was never an important issue in Wilmington politics even during the mid-1850s when the American Party, the political manifes-

[10] *Ibid.,* 1900, 1:612.
[11] U.S. Census, 1904, *Occupations,* pp. 758–61.

tation of a local Know-Nothing lodge, controlled the state government for a brief period.[12] Neither did the city ever fall prey to rioting prompted by ethnic bigotry such as afflicted Philadelphia in the 1840s.[13] Throughout the nineteenth century immigrants were not segregated in ghettos—at least not at the ward level—but were spread throughout the city's twelve wards in the same proportions as was the population generally.[14] The scattered locations of the city's Roman Catholic churches suggest a similar conclusion. In the early twentieth century when Polish and Italian immigrants began arriving in Wilmington, they settled in enclaves in the then developing south and southwest parts of Wilmington, thus establishing a pattern of ethnic clustering that was new to the city.[15]

Although no Irish or German immigrants rose to prominence as industrialists or were admitted into the top social circle of the city as described by Canby, it was not unusual for persons of foreign birth to achieve success and respectability in such professions as journalism, real estate, and construction, not to mention brewing and saloon keeping. St. Mary's College prepared a number of local Catholic youths for professional careers during the 1850s and 1860s and no doubt provided a more genteel image of Catholic culture to Protestant and Catholic Wilmingtonians than was common in many American communities.

While religious and ethnic bigotry caused few problems in Wilmington, racism had a more divisive influence on community life. Throughout the second half of the nineteenth century the percentage of black people in Wilmington's population hovered around 10 percent. The "darkies" in their back street shanties, who impinged so little upon Canby's youthful vision, accounted for 7,677 of Wilmington's 61,431 people in 1890.[16] Unlike the large cities of the Northeast and Midwest where immigrants made up the most significant groups living in a culture of poverty, blacks constituted Wilmington's largest minority group. Debarred as they were from entrance into the trade unions, the opportunities for blacks to become skilled

---

[12] Charles H. Bohner, "Rum and Reform," *Delaware History* 5 (1953): 263.

[13] Sam B. Warner, *The Private City*, pp. 125–57.

[14] U.S. Census, 1890, *Population*, 1:526.

[15] *Ibid.*, 1910, 2:283.

[16] *Ibid.*, 1890, 1:704.

workers actually declined in the course of the nineteenth century. This factor militated against their achieving mobility in an economy that emphasized industrial skills. Consequently, in spite of the city's belated efforts at providing "separate but equal" educational facilities, the number of blacks who rose above the status of casual laborers was miniscule.

Racism kept blacks political vassals of the Republican party and allowed politicians to ignore meaningful local issues while engaging in Negro baiting. The local Democratic party, which attracted migrants from lower Delaware and many immigrants from abroad, was a self-proclaimed white man's party. By contrast the Republicans depended upon black votes to win local elections. Election campaigns were nearly always the scenes of racial incidents. The most serious riot in post-Civil War Wilmington's history occurred in 1880 when nine hundred marchers in a Democratic parade attacked a group of blacks in front of a black lodge hall. Seventeen whites and six blacks were injured by stones and shotgun or revolver fire before police could restore order.[17] The normal democratic process by which a minority group is able to gain political power at the ballot box in order to secure patronage and other political benefits was frustrated in the case of blacks because the Republicans were under no pressure to bargain for their support. Few blacks received patronage jobs and only one served on the police force during the last thirty years of the century.[18] In addition to being thus barred from economic or political advancement, blacks were also excluded from participation in many community activities and entertainments. One trolley company advertised that its trolleymen were instructed not to pick up black passengers.[19]

As we have seen, black Wilmingtonians tried to adapt to urbanization and industrialization in many of the same ways that whites did. They formed churches that became important organizations in the community for self-help and fellowship. They organized lodges and clubs. Despite the poverty that prevailed among blacks and the absence of compulsory school legislation, more than 40 percent of the city's black children attended elementary school. The evidence indicates that in the post-Civil War period the example of the white world's associational urban culture suggested the only route

[17] *Wilmington Morning News,* Oct. 18, 1880.
[18] *Every Evening,* Feb. 21, 1891.
[19] Weslager, *Brandywine Springs,* p. 88.

118

by which black people could attain respectability. But whites were unwilling to respect blacks regardless of their efforts toward cultural assimilation.

The Nature of the City's Industries

As the board of trade proclaimed in its promotional literature, strikes and labor violence were as rare in Wilmington as were violent ethnic disputes. Unlike some other industrial cities such as Paterson, New Jersey, and Lawrence, Massachusetts, which employed large numbers of immigrants as unskilled factory laborers, Wilmington's foundries and car- and shipbuilding companies needed a high percentage of skilled workers.[20] There were, of course, some Wilmington factories that employed many unskilled workers, cotton mills, a fertilizer factory, a match factory, and the tanneries, but none of these industries were strong enough in Wilmington to have a dominant impact on the general composition of the city's working force. This is an important factor to keep in mind since labor militancy in the nineteenth century was to a considerable degree a function of the declining importance of skilled labor in American industry and the concomitant rapid growth through natural increase and immigration of the pool of unskilled labor. Consequently militancy was often associated with concentrations of low-skilled industries, as in one-industry textile towns.

Mechanization did not greatly affect the demand for skilled labor in Wilmington. Power equipment was introduced into such industries as carriage making and car building to accelerate routine tasks or to help in the lifting and positioning of heavy objects in the assembly process, but these technological innovations did not reduce the need for carpenters, upholsterers, iron casters, and painters. The men who performed these skilled jobs saw themselves, and were seen by society, as the principal upholders of the city's economy. In most instances the owners of the companies that employed them had themselves sprung from the ranks of skilled workers. Strikes among these elite members of the working class were rare. It is noteworthy, by contrast, that the one lengthy strike in the last thirty years of the century was among the tanners, the only large industry in Wilmington

[20] See Patrick Renshaw, *The Wobblies*, pp. 133–56.

57. *An Example of Wilmington Woodwork Design.* Dresser with mirror built by carpenters at the Jackson & Sharp Company for installation in a private railroad car. (Courtesy E.M.H.L.)

that relied upon unskilled workers. Company-owned housing and other paternalistic practices that were features of the early water-powered industries along the Brandywine were unknown among the steam-powered Christina-based industries of the mid- and late century. The newer firms did, however, encourage their better-paid skilled workers to buy homes in the city through contributary building and loan associations. Seventeen such associations existed in 1869, the period of their greatest popularity.[21] Thus, by a calculated policy that they freely admitted, the business leaders attempted to dampen labor militancy by encouraging a stake-in-society psychology among workingmen and involving them in mortgage payments. As the figures in the Appendix show, this approach was none too successful because the majority of Wilmingtonians were not homeowners, but neither were they paying rent to the men they worked for as were industrial workers in some other cities such as Pullman, Illinois.

The development of labor organization in Wilmington was greatly influenced by its proximity to Philadelphia, a city that was in the forefront of nineteenth-century American unionization. In 1829 some Wilmington artisans founded the Association of Working People of New Castle County along lines suggested by the Philadelphia Mechanics' Union of Trade to lobby for legislation to abolish chartered monopolies and imprisonment for debt, and to enact a mechanics lien law and free public education.[22] The association was similar to other so-called workingmen's organizations of the Jacksonian Era in that its members were self-employed artisans, not factory hands, and its goals were political and social as well as economic. Because public opinion was already favorably disposed toward the major reforms sought by the association, the organization was short-lived.

Following the association's demise, the next important effort to organize the workingmen in Wilmington was made during the 1840s by the Order of the United American Mechanics, a fraternal order founded in Philadelphia in 1845.[23] The United Mechanics, which appealed to skilled workers, provided members with death and sickness benefits and aid in securing work as well as opportunities to socialize. The order became an important social agency for working people and remained a strong organization in

[21] *Every Evening*, Oct. 16, 1872.
[22] Thomas R. Dew, "Delaware's First Labor Party," p. 1.
[23] *Blue Hen's Chicken*, June 29, 1849; *Every Evening*, Feb. 28, 1873.

Wilmington throughout the nineteenth century, but it was never a pressure group either politically or as a labor union. A similar group, the Morocco Dressers Union of Friendship and Benevolence, was instituted in Wilmington in 1858. Like the Mechanics, it offered its members health and life insurance, and it sponsored social evenings, including an annual ball.[24]

Labor unions did not appear in Wilmington until the movement toward large factories, begun during the 1840s, became the city's predominent industrial form. Whereas many of the owners of Wilmington's foundries, car and carriage shops, and tanneries rose from the ranks of skilled workmen, in the 1860s and 1870s it became increasingly common for men with office experience or for sons of owners, some with college degrees in engineering, to take over the leadership of Wilmington's major firms. A notable example of the new-style executives was J. Taylor Gause, who rose to the presidency of Harlan & Hollingsworth after the deaths of the firm's artisan-founders. Gause, probably the most influential industrial leader in Wilmington during the final third of the nineteenth century, had an academy education; his previous work experience at Harlan's had been in the office. Gause maintained tight control over the hundreds of workmen at the city's largest car- and shipbuilding company. In a magazine interview in 1872 he declared that his firm "never had any trouble" with labor dispute because of his method for "nipping sea-lawyers in the bud." The "sea-lawyer," he explained, "is the calculating, dissatisfied man. A supposed grievance arises, the men have their meeting, and the sea-lawyer begins to stir them up, big in his opportunity. We find who he is, pay him on the instant, and send him away. The men run about for awhile with their complaints in their heads, but with nobody to utter them by. It ends by their coming to us in a body to receive back the mischiefmaker, by this time repentant. This we generally do, getting a friend converted from an enemy."[25]

Gause's easy assumption of employer control over the workingman had

[24] *Delaware State Journal,* June 24, 1859; Dec. 30, 1862.
[25] *Harkness Magazine,* 5:353.

---

58. *The Interior of a Parlor Car.* An example of the meticulous work required in the carbuilding industry. (Courtesy E.M.H.L.)

59. *John Taylor Gause (1823–1898). A Semi-Centennial Memoir of the Harlan & Hollingsworth Company*, opp. p. 156. (Courtesy E.M.H.L.)

60. *The Managers of the Harlan & Hollingsworth Company.* J. T. Gause is seated in the center. *A Semi-Centennial Memoir of the Harlan & Hollingsworth Company*, opp. p. 305. (Courtesy E.M.H.L.)

much to justify it in the 1870s, a depression decade. But even in that era of relative calm, some local men were seeking new approaches to labor-management relations. Most of these efforts proved to be fruitless in the short run, but they provided the groundwork for more extensive employee demands in the 1880s. Stirrings of labor restlessness came to Wilmington during the late 1860s and early 1870s when the eight-hour movement attracted much attention, gained a following, and then declined. The coachmakers union first aired the demand for shorter hours in 1865 at a well-attended public meeting. They proposed that the various trades should form unions to agitate for the eight-hour day, and the meeting adopted a resolution to the effect that longer hours of work rendered men unfit to head their households.[26] The movement did not catch hold, however, and it was not until 1872 that another effort was made, this time in the form of an Eight Hour League. Similar leagues appeared in other American cities at that time to arouse public support for the shorter day, and speakers from the New York league visited Wilmington in support of the reform. Once again Wilmington's working population failed to retain its enthusiasm for the movement and few turned out to join the proposed league.

A sign of contemporary recognition of the apparent decline of mobility and growing differences between blue-collar and white-collar life-styles was the appearance of cultural institutions designed to raise working-class aspirations. In 1869 representatives of business, labor, and the professions inaugurated a workingmen's institute in an effort to provide opportunities

Another means of improving the workingmen's lot, which attracted attention in the early 1870s, was the cooperative factory. The idea was for several skilled workingmen to pool their financial resources and start their own factory. Ten journeymen morocco finishers began Mullan, Dougherty & Company,[27] while another group of mechanics raised enough money through stock subscriptions to begin a car works in Oxford, Pennsylvania.[28] The cooperative movement was not extensive, however, and while it provided an opportunity for a few persons to rise from employee to employer status, it did not alter the relationships between these two groups since the coops hired hands on exactly the same basis as did other firms.

[26] *Delaware State Journal,* Oct. 20, 1865.
[27] *Every Evening,* July 3, 1872.
[28] *Ibid.,* Apr. 24, 1873; Aug. 14, 1873.

of self-improvement for industrial workers. Reverend Fielder Israel of the city's Unitarian Church conceived of the institute as a place for recreation and lectures and as a job information bureau and library. During its first year the institute sponsored several lectures, mostly on technical and scientific subjects, intended to broaden the workingman's understanding of the principles which underlay industrial production. Membership was free; the costs were paid by subscriptions from its middle-class sponsors, but the institute was never well financed and quickly declined in importance.[29] Its decline attests to the chasm between what middle-class philanthropists thought was good for the workingman and what workmen really desired.

Socialism made its first appearance in Wilmington in May 1878 when an estimated two hundred people, mostly workingmen, turned out to hear George G. Block of Philadelphia speak at a meeting sponsored by the local Liberal League. The league, made up principally of Unitarians, had heretofore confined its activities to providing a platform for speakers who held unusual religious opinions. Block argued that the problem of the American economy was surplus labor, which drove down wages. He argued that shorter hours—not cheaper money, as the Greenback party claimed—could remedy this situation, and he urged Wilmington's workers to form a Socialist party and establish a newspaper to promote reform. About thirty people at the meeting signed up for the new party. There followed a brief flurry of interest in socialism in Wilmington, confined mostly to the German community.[30] The movement never gained sufficient momentum to make either Germans or socialism seem really threatening.

As the effects of the depression diminished, strikes became more common in Wilmington's industries, but strikers were seldom successful because scabs from the Philadelphia-Camden area were readily available. For example, when forty pebblers at the Washington Jones Morocco Company walked off the job in 1878 demanding a wage increase from eight to nine dollars per week, the company had little difficulty finding replacements.[31] Similarly, when workers at the Malleable Iron Company struck in 1885 to protest new work rules forbidding them to come to work early to socialize, the company found substitutes immediately.

[29] *Ibid.*, Feb. 15, 1872.
[30] *Ibid.*, May 9, 1878; May 31, 1878.
[31] *Ibid.*, Feb. 18, 1878.

126

Wilmington's high-water mark for union activities and strikes occurred in 1885 and 1886, yet even at that time of intense feeling there was no violence or polarization in the city. It was the heyday of the Knights of Labor, founded by a Philadelphia tailor's cutter in 1869 as a secret union for all working people. The Knights introduced an assembly in Wilmington during the late 1870s. Its first local successes were among workers at the shipyards and machine shops along the Christina. By 1879 the new union appeared to be on the wane, however, when its secrets were revealed by half-initiate members.[32] Subsequently, as the Knights expanded elsewhere, they seemed to disappear in Wilmington, thus giving credence to local industrialists' claims of labor docility. Wilmington appeared to be a haven for companies threatened by unionization. Out of this situation came Wilmington's greatest strike, the morocco workers' walkout of 1886, which illustrates better than any other incident the restrained approach to labor disputes that generally prevailed among workers and factory owners alike in Wilmington.

The trouble started when Clerk & Lennox Morrocco Company of Haverhill, Massachusetts, refused to honor a union demand to fire a foreman who had proved a traitor to the Knights by divulging their secrets. Rather than fight it out with the union in Haverhill, where the Knights were strong, Clerk & Lennox chose to relocate in Wilmington, Delaware, in 1885, where they had been assured that the Knights were ineffectual. The Haverhill assembly informed local union leaders of the reason for the move, and the word spread quickly through Wilmington.[33] It also became known that the firm planned to pay its Wilmington workers less than it had been accustomed to paying in the New England city. Local morocco workers were aroused. Because Wilmington's reputation for low wages was galling to them, when local Knights representatives called upon the company's local employees to strike pending the removal of the Haverhill foreman, one half of the Wilmington personnel of Clerk & Lennox walked off the job. To dramatize their demands, the Knights hired a boy to picket the Clerk & Lennox factory. He was arrested for inciting to riot, but a Wilmington judge dismissed the case. Several other pickets joined with the boy and the Knights made good use of the strike at Clerk & Lennox to recruit new mem-

[32] *Ibid.*, Mar. 6, 1879.
[33] *Ibid.*, Oct. 5, 1885.

bers. Speakers from Philadelphia and New York assemblies urged the many workmen who attended a meeting at the Opera House to join the union. Working people, especially in the morocco factories, flocked to join the organization, and in December 1885 the Leather Workers' Assembly, Knights of Labor made a public show of strength when 166 couples attended their first annual ball. Forty couples came down from the Philadelphia assembly as guests of the Wilmington union, an indication that the Philadelphia group was anxious to strengthen ties with their fellow workers in the smaller city down river.[34] By February 1886 the Knights were planning to erect a large hall in Wilmington to accommodate their growing assemblies. In March the *Every Evening*, the city's most popular daily newspaper, reported that "the Knights of Labor, by the thoroughness and rapidity with which they are organizing and gaining members in this city and state, are attracting the bulk of public attention at the present time. The membership of the order in this city alone is put at 10,000 men."[35] The paper went on to explain that the order was composed of assemblies representing the various trades. Each assembly sent three delegates to the district assembly, which for Wilmington was in Philadelphia. The district assemblies in turn sent delegates to the national general assembly. Some local Knights were worried by the meteoric rise of the organization in Wilmington. They feared that some new members might assume that the increasing membership was a prelude to a grand strike, when in fact the chief principle underlying the Knights of Labor was the advantage of arbitration over strikes as a means toward adjusting labor disputes.

At first it appeared that these fears were unfounded. The *Sunday Star* editor prophesied that the Knights would improve labor-management relations.[36] At the Jackson & Sharp car works, which was suffering from the competition of George Pullman's Illinois plant, employees were gratified to discover that unionization had made management more candid with them about the company's problems. To preserve a competitive status, Job Jackson had replaced set wage schedules with piece-work rates that cut the company's manufacturing costs. When the men complained about their pay cut, Jackson told them that he wished that he could pay them all enough

[34] *Ibid.*, Dec. 19, 1885.
[35] *Ibid.*, Mar. 4, 1886.
[36] *Sunday Star*, Mar. 21, 1886.

61. *Job H. Jackson (1833–1901).
Every Evening History of Wilmington.* (Courtesy E.M.H.L.)

so that they could have comfortable homes and could provide their children
with good educations. But, he said, the Pullman Company's price-cutting
had reduced Jackson & Sharp's orders. Jackson had promised committees of
workers who met with him to increase wages as soon as orders for cars war-
ranted it. Yet, despite his forthrightness, he complained, the local Knights
had invited a committee of Knights from Philadelphia to meet with him.
Jackson regarded this step as unfair and objected to outside interference.
Already the threat of labor trouble had cost the firm contracts. He reiterated
that he was willing to work with the Knights as long as they represented his
own workers, but he refused to be pressured by union leaders from outside
Wilmington. After Jackson had finished speaking he entertained questions.
Apparently the men were convinced by his sincerity, and the rumored strike
did not materialize.[37]

Harlan & Hollingsworth took a firmer line toward the union movement, as
was their custom. Just two weeks after Jackson's speech, Harlan's turned
down a lucrative contract to build two ferryboats. According to a company

[37] *Every Evening,* Mar. 8, 1886; Mar. 12, 1886.

129

62. *Parlor of the Jackson Home, Decorated for Job Jackson's 50th Birthday Celebration, February 1883.* Jackson & Sharp employees sent their president a gold watch and the *Every Evening* remarked on the cordial relations that Jackson enjoyed with his workers that were "too often the exception in the large establishments." *Every Evening*, February 13, 1883. (Courtesy A.S.D.)

spokesman, "in view of the possibility of there being a general labor agitation throughout the country during the summer and especially on account of the uncertainty which exists in industrial circles, owing to the unreasonable demands which are being made by the workmen, we deem it wise not to fill up our works with contracts at this time. . . ." To a reporter's query about the company's attitude toward the Knights the spokesman replied, "We do not object to our men joining the order if they think it to their interest to do so. We do not discriminate against the members of any society." But, he continued, "it is a well known fact that all the agitation in regard to labor matters comes from the inferior grades of workman—those who have nothing at stake, have never served their apprenticeships, and who are not skillful enough at their trades to earn more than the minimum pay. The most unfortunate feature of the present crusade of the Knights of Labor is that the better class of mechanics and those who own their own houses and have property and other interests at stake are drawn into the organization. . . . They lose their identity and become the victims of more designing men, who are thereafter at liberty to order them out on a strike regardless of the personal loss they inevitably suffer."[38] The "sea-lawyers" were growing more clever and secretive, and J. T. Gause was prepared for trouble.

In the meantime events were moving toward a climax in the morocco industry, where the Knights' agitation had begun. On March 23 the *Every Evening* reported that the Knights were calling a strike against Wilmington's morocco companies because the executives of these firms had failed to appear at a meeting that the assembly leaders had requested. Immediately upon the announcement of the strike, morocco workers poured out of their factories and headed for Institute Hall at Eighth and Market streets, where they met under strict security to discuss the situation. About seven hundred people—men and women, black and white—attended the secret meeting chaired by assembly leader Matthew Colwell, who had been Wilmington's most active Knight from the time of the Clark & Lennox affair.[39]

Unlike the carbuilders, the morocco manufacturers organized to meet the strike as a group. All belonged to the national Morocco Manufacturers Association and its president was a Wilmingtonian, General J. Parke Postles. Pos-

[38] *Ibid.*, Mar. 20, 1886.
[39] *Ibid.*, Mar. 23, 1886.

tles, a Civil War hero and sometime Democratic politician, held a meeting of his fellow manufacturers on the day following the strike call, after which the owners issued a statement to the effect that they had not felt obliged to attend the talks suggested by the knights because the union had not forwarded any specific demands beforehand. The manufacturers said that they suspected that the local assembly was being used by "outsiders," and they therefore refused to have any further dealings with the Knights of Labor. The manufacturers announced that they were prepared for a long strike and would close down operations.[40]

It was soon evident that the national Morocco Manufacturers Association was anything but a united group. Wage demands were the major obstacle to a rapid settlement of the strike. The Wilmington morocco tanneries paid lower wages than their counterparts in Philadelphia. The Wilmington manufacturers argued that a low wage policy was necessary to the survival of the industry in the smaller city because, unlike the Philadelphia tanners, who had a ready market in nearby shoe factories and binderies, the Wilmington firms sold most of their products outside this city in Philadelphia, Boston, and in the midwestern centers of the boot and shoe industry. As General Postles put it, "the manufacturers of Philadelphia have a constant market at their very door; their wheelbarrow trade is a big lift. That is a big factor in our ability to pay, or to have our goods cost as much as they do in Philadelphia. You know that bricklayers and other tradesmen get more in Philadelphia than they do here and still more in New York. They live cheaper in Philadelphia than in New York, still cheaper here, and cheaper yet in smaller towns and villages. If you make a uniform rate of wages you blot out the wayside places."[41] Wilmington was a jobbing market. In order to entice buyers from the big boot and shoe plants and other companies that used morocco, her prices had to be cheaper than those offered by tanneries in the cities that had large leather-using industries. Postles and the other Wilmington manufacturers suspected that their counterparts in Philadelphia who had the most to gain from a strike in Wilmington were maneuvering behind the scenes through the Philadelphia district assembly to prolong the strike in Wilmington.

The manufacturers and the union leadership held several fruitless meet-

[40] *Ibid.,* Mar. 24, 1886.
[41] *Ibid.,* Apr. 1, 1886.

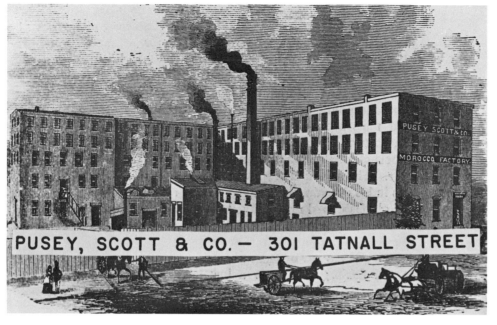

63. *A Wilmington Morocco Factory.* Engraving taken from A. J. Clement, *Wilmington, Delaware, Its Productive Industries and Commercial and Maritime Advantages* (Wilmington, 1888), p. 35. (Courtesy E.M.H.L.)

ings at which the companies refused the union demand to raise wages in line with those paid in Philadelphia and the strike dragged on. Postles tried unsuccessfully to effect a meeting between the Philadelphia members of the National Morocco Manufacturers Association and the Wilmington manufacturers.[42] Only a few local manufacturers dealt independently with their workers to reach settlements. Most were determined to negotiate as a group. Some strikers left Wilmington for jobs in Philadelphia, Trenton, Newark, and Brooklyn as the strike entered its second month. The majority, however, waited it out, subsisting on strike fund payments of six to eight dollars a week, which were in part collected from the Philadelphia and New England branches of the Knights of Labor. Wilmington Knights also busied themselves with plans to build their own morocco factory to be managed on a cooperative basis.[43]

[42] *Ibid.*, Apr. 1, 1886.
[43] *Ibid.*, Apr. 2, 1886; Apr. 17, 1886; Apr. 20, 1886; Apr. 30, 1886.

Wilmington, Delaware   The long morocco strike generated great community interest. Local newspapers carried fresh reports about it every day. The prevailing editorial opinion seemed to favor the manufacturers, who were pictured as bargaining in good faith against the stacked deck of Philadelphia involvement.[44] But there was no sign of panic, no fear of disorder. In the midst of the strike the sensational Haymarket bombings took place in Chicago. Wilmington editors reacted with a stream of invective against "the socialist rioters of Chicago" whose actions brought threats of "anarchy."[45] The dramatic events in Chicago, however, failed to disperse the community's calm acceptance of its own strikers whose actions the press described as well-intentioned but ill-considered. That Wilmington was not polarized can be seen from the open-minded attitudes with which many local industrialists continued to regard the problems of workingmen. About the time of the Chicago disturbances a number of Wilmington's leading manufacturers in various industries attended a meeting to discuss labor troubles. The major speaker, George W. Stone, took the position that the substitution of machinery for hand labor, which had characterized the preceding generation, had improved everyone's standard of living, but had simultaneously permitted a few men to gain too much wealth and power. Stock manipulators were the ones really responsible for the unreasonable attitude being taken by labor organizations, he explained. Stone warned that unless the unions curbed their current demands for revenge, they would lose the public's sympathy.[46] Judging from the questions asked by several manufacturers after the talk, it would appear that they accepted his theory of the cause of the crisis between labor and management. The attitudes of Wilmington capitalists were formed in the light of their own sense of being somewhat outside what was coming to be the mainstream of industrial power in the United States, and as much as any union leader they resented the predominance of larger, more efficient firms in Chicago, Philadelphia, and other big cities. In addition, Wilmington still had among its manufacturers a number of Quakers or men with Quaker backgrounds who viewed the worker-owner relationship as one of cooperation, not conflict. These men were un-

[44] *Sunday Star,* Mar. 28, 1886.
[45] *Every Evening,* May 5, 1886.
[46] *Ibid.,* Apr. 29, 1886.

134

comfortable with the increasing pressures in the American economy that emphasized profits at whatever cost. Paternalism had been in a state of steady erosion in Wilmington since the introduction of steam power, but it was not completely dead.

Meanwhile the strike continued through the summer of 1886. In August the strikers put their case before the national executive board of the Knights of Labor. The morocco manufacturers agreed to discuss the strike with Terence Powderly's board on condition that such meetings would not be construed as constituting binding arbitration.[47] A meeting between Powderly and Postles did take place, but to no avail since sluggish market conditions put the manufacturers under no pressure to resume tanning.[48] Those few manufacturers who did wish to recommence production purchased additional labor-saving machines and hired scabs without arousing any labor violence.[49] As the strike continued, employers became more insistent on bargaining with their own employees directly rather than through the Knights of Labor. By the first week in October, the strikers were reported to be quietly going back to work after having been idle for twenty-seven weeks. The strike was officially ended in mid-October by an order of the executive board of District 94 of the Knights of Labor. The defeated board informed the strikers that they would have to negotiate for jobs individually, but that the employers had promised the board that they would not discriminate against the strikers. At the time the strike collapsed only an estimated 390 of the original 950 morocco workers were still on strike, the majority had either returned to work in one of the few Wilmington factories that settled independently, or had gone elsewhere to find work.[50]

Subsequently the Knights of Labor declined in Wilmington. Having lost a strike here under the most promising conditions possible, with a large strike fund, much outside support, and worker solidarity, workingmen had little reason to hope that the union could be effective in the future. When in 1890 the National Morocco Manufacturers Association agreed that members should fire all Knights in their employ, the union quietly dropped

[47] *Ibid.*, Aug. 3, 1886.
[48] *Ibid.*, Aug. 23, 1886.
[49] *Ibid.*, Sept. 10, 1886.
[50] *Ibid.*, Oct. 16, 1886.

Wilmington,
Delaware

out of the morocco industry.[51] Labor-management relations in Wilmington returned to their pre-Knights pattern of scattered walkouts, mostly in the textile mills, that frequently left the workers' grievances unresolved.

A most interesting strike with regard to working conditions in the post-morocco period occurred in 1887 at Harlan & Hollingsworth's over the issue of the company's hiring of female painters to do work once reserved for men. Women were hired to paint the interiors of boats while men continued to paint the exteriors. Men were paid nine to twelve dollars a week, whereas women worked the same hours for five to seven dollars. The men accepted the new situation until inevitable April showers prevented their working out of doors. Faced with layoffs, the men wrote a letter of complaint to President J. T. Gause, pointing out that in the old days they had painted interiors on rainy days. He replied in his usual brusk fashion, saying that they should either accept the loss of interior work or draw their time. Twenty-nine of the thirty-one boatyard painters took the latter course. They were easily replaced by men who would accept the female work team.[52]

A restive quiet marked Wilmington labor through the last decade of the century. Craft unions were more conspicuous in Labor Day parades and picnics than in negotiations with employers. The major labor disputes that plagued the nation during the depressed 1890s had few repercussions in Wilmington. When the Pullman strike in Illinois brought widespread sympathy walkouts in the railroad industry, Wilmington railroad employees stayed on the job. Even George Pullman's Wilmington shops, the company's large east-coast facility, continued as usual throughout the course of the strike against his Illinois plant.[53] Another index of labor impotence in the 1890s was the fruitless effort of the United Labor League to secure state laws restricting child labor, factory inspection, and workmen's compensation.[54]

The turn of the century ushered in the reforming breeze of the progressive movement. A new spirit of middle-class sympathy for the plight of the working class and recognition that government intervention was necessary to achieve acceptable standards made possible reforms that had been un-

[51] *Ibid.,* Nov. 1, 1890.
[52] *Ibid.,* Apr. 9, 1887.
[53] *Ibid.,* July 10, 1894.
[54] *Ibid.,* Feb. 16, 1895; Apr. 6, 1897.

136

64. *A Travelling Show Car*. The mural work on the sides of this Jackson & Sharp-built car, illustrates the specialized painting that could be produced by Wilmington car shops. (Courtesy E.M.H.L.)

achievable a decade earlier. The state legislature adopted a factory-inspection act that required employers to provide separate washrooms for female employees and to keep females "reasonably and comfortably warm" in factories. These meager provisions were to be enforced by a female inspector who reported annually to the chief justice of the Delaware Supreme Court. She was permitted to recommend additional safety and health restrictions, but she had no powers of enforcement.[55] The factory-inspection law was a first step, however small, toward increased government involvement in industry. The factory inspector could command a public platform from which she could request additional legislation. Her efforts to promote the restriction of child labor were rewarded in 1905 with the adoption of a law that prevented children under fourteen from working in factories, and required young people between the ages of fourteen and sixteen to attend school at least part time if they worked. In Wilmington the new law affected morocco factories and hosiery mills, which employed the largest number among the 919 children under sixteen listed as workers in the 1900 census.[56] But a study in 1910 revealed that the law was flagrantly violated.[57]

The middle-class public's increased sympathy for the workingman was displayed most notably in the course of the machinists' strike in 1901. This strike grew out of the efforts of the International Association of Machinists to bring Wilmington's working hours into line with those of New York and other large east-coast cities.[58] The international union feared that if Wilmington machine and shipbuilding companies did not shorten the workday to nine hours, their competitors in New York and elsewhere would restore longer hours to remain competitive. Samuel Gompers personally came to Wilmington to launch the drive. After a series of meetings, the union succeeded in attracting many new members.[59] In May 1901, 350 Wilmington machinists struck against six companies. Pusey & Jones, Lobdell's, Edgemoor Bridge Company, and a few machine shops accepted the nine-hour day and were therefore unaffected.[60] Among the recalcitrant firms, the largest were Harlan & Hollingsworth and J. Morton Poole Company. Harlan & Hollingsworth notified their 110 striking machinists that they must return to work or face dismissal.[61] The painters and drill-press operators at Harlan's then struck in sympathy with the machinists. As the

[55] *Ibid.,* Aug. 31, 1903.
[56] U.S. Census, 1900, *Occupations,* p. 756.
[57] *Report Concerning Conditions of Toilers,* Diocese of Delaware, 1910, W.I.F.L. Collection.
[58] *Every Evening,* Apr. 12, 1901.
[59] *Sunday Star,* Apr. 28, 1901.
[60] *Every Evening,* May, 20, 1901; May 21, 1901.
[61] *Ibid.,* May 25, 1901; *Sunday Star,* July 14, 1901.

strike wore on into the late spring and summer, clergymen of various denominations praised the strikers for their orderly behavior.[62] The machinists were feted with entertainment, speeches and baseball games, as public opinion strongly supported their demands. Harlan & Hollingsworth executives were unimpressed by the holiday spirit of the affair. Having already suffered some sympathy walkouts, they feared more defections. The company requested police protection to prevent the men on strike from intimidating those still at work. Police bullying of employees did not improve company morale.[63] A few days after the police arrived, the company hired detectives from Philadelphia whose revolvers made the workers more uncomfortable still. These steps, although they proved to be an unnecessary overreaction, did not lead to additional trouble. In mid-July, seven weeks after the strike began, the machinists agreed to return to a sixty-hour work week at Harlan's, in return for a dollar per week raise in pay.[64] In Wilmington, as throughout the nation at the turn of the century, there was labor discontent but that discontent did not polarize the city along class lines to the same extent as occurred in places where violence accompanied labor agitation.

The Philanthropic Ladies

One of the most notable new factors in the dynamics of social development in the post-1870 period was the growth of private philanthropies linked to the coming of age of the children of the city's industrial pioneers and the greater involvement of women in community activities. The second generation of industrial leaders fell natural heirs to community leadership. Better educated than their parents and more remote from working-class life, they were no less committed than their parents' generation had been to raising the cultural level of their city and mitigating its various social problems. The means employed by the younger generation to achieve these ends were

[62] *Ibid.*, June 4, 1901; June 8, 1901.
[63] *Ibid.*, June 11, 1901.
[64] *Sunday Star,* July 14, 1901.

more highly coordinated than in the past and depended more on secular rather than church-related organization. Although the philanthropies of this era have been criticized for their "Lady Bountiful" style, they were a distinct improvement over previous welfare efforts. Privately organized welfare agencies grew dramatically in size, number, and scope during the later years of the century. In part this development was prompted by misfortunes brought on by the Civil War and by the ability and desire of affluent Wilmingtonians to meet the needs of different categories of unfortunates such as unwed mothers, orphans, and impoverished widows by establishing institutional homes for them. The wives and daughters of the city's manufacturers and professional men formed the backbone of the two most important and broad-based philanthropic agencies created in the city in these years, the Associated Charities and the New Century Club.

The morality of charity work posed one of the great American dilemmas of the late-nineteenth century as the conflict between the individual needs of a volatile industrial economy clashed with a philosophy that rigidly identified morality with individual self-help. Like their counterparts elsewhere, many well-to-do Wilmingtonians felt uneasy about the rise of socialistic doctrines such as Henry George's single tax and the continual menace of tramps and vagabonds who begged food at kitchen doors and camped in groups on the outskirts of the city. For most of the nineteenth century the only organized relief for unemployed or unemployable people was the county almshouse. The only sources of ongoing outdoor relief were the churches. This haphazard method of almsgiving was both inefficient and unfair since some people contrived to get aid from more than one source. Out of these conflicting attitudes and needs came Associated Charities, an agency that attempted to organize the city's charitable enterprises on a rational basis.

The first step toward permanent citywide cooperation among charities came in the depression winter of 1874 when a group of concerned citizens formed an ad hoc committee to solicit funds for distribution to an estimated two thousand jobless men.[65] One permanent agency emerged from this effort, the Young Ladies Relief Society, a group of forty girls and young matrons. Convinced that the poor should be given work rather than a dole, the

[65] *Every Evening,* Dec. 17, 1874.

140

Young Ladies opened a permanent reading room for working girls and a sewing room for jobless women.[66] Those who became caught up in this philanthropic work were sorely aware of the limited nature of their efforts and thus in 1884, together with other local volunteer welfare workers, they formed an enthusiastic audience for a speech by Mrs. Charles G. Ames, president of the Children's Aid Society of Philadelphia, on the subject of the cooperative efforts of the charities in that city. Mrs. Ames told how Philadelphia charity workers had consolidated their diverse charities and established a system called "friendly visiting," whereby volunteers called on the poor to investigate applications for aid and to suggest means toward home economy.[67] Shortly thereafter, following a series of public meetings, representatives of Wilmington's charitable organizations, led by Emalea Pusey Warner, president of the Young Ladies Society, met to form the Associated Charities. Mrs. Warner was the wife of Alfred D. Warner, an officer in his family's shipping firm, and the daughter of Lea Pusey, a Quaker manufacturer and supporter of innumerable civic causes.[68] She proved to be the most dynamic and unflagging advocate of social work in Wilmington during the next generation. Hers was the moving spirit that sustained the association movement.

The new organization was not designed to replace the existing charities but to coordinate them. Its founders hoped to eliminate duplication among agencies and to provide alternatives to the dole. They were inspired by the belief that persons asking for handouts could be readily separated into two groups, "the poor," those who strive toward self-support but might be in temporary need because of illness or some other cause beyond their control, and "paupers," those who shamelessly sought a dole in lieu of working.[69] The new charity organizers divided the city into districts and appointed a committee of six to twelve lady visitors to investigate requests for relief in each district. The association hired a professional superintendant to oversee its other work, which included the administration of a woodpile where male applicants could work for their pay just as females were required to do by sewing, and the distribution of coal and groceries to needy

[66] *Ibid.*, Sept. 15, 1877.
[67] *Ibid.*, Feb. 7, 1885.
[68] Emalea P. Warner, *Childhood Memories* (Wilmington, Del., 1939), p. 5.
[69] *Every Evening*, Oct. 28, 1884.

65. *Emalea Pusey Warner, Leading
Social Worker.* (Courtesy Mrs.
Stephen A. Trentman)

families. Otherwise the association did not provide aid but rather referred cases to existing agencies such as the almshouse or the Female Benevolent Society. The association's activities in 1886 suggest the scope of its work. In that year, a prosperous one for Wilmington's businesses, the friendly visitors received 1,802 applications for relief, only 130 of which were from vagrants or nonresidents. The association filled 838 coal orders, 486 grocery orders, and 151 medical prescriptions, and referred 260 white and 214 Negro families to other charities, which gave them "substantial aid." The association accomplished all of this on a budget of $3,864.97, nearly a third of which went toward the salary of the superintendent. These funds came as gifts from individuals and businesses.[70]

As the years passed and as they gained experience with the conditions of poverty, the ladies who managed the Associated Charities enlarged the scope of their activities. During the 1890s they contracted with nearby farmers to take in poor families for a week's vacation in the country. Their campaign for improvements in the care of the state's wards and pris-

[70] *Annual Report, Associated Charities,* 1886.

oners resulted in a law prohibiting children's being placed in the almshouse and in the erection of a new county workhouse. Another foray into
politics in 1904 secured a compulsory school law over the bitter opposition
of some farmers and industrial employers of children. They hired a visiting
nurse who investigated sanitation problems and reported her findings to the
board of health. In 1888 they started a day nursery for the benefit of working mothers and began a program to encourage the poor to cultivate vege-
tables in vacant lots around the city. Prior to the establishment of a YWCA,
the Associated Charities maintained a boardinghouse for working girls
and gave cooking and sewing classes in poor neighborhoods.[71] The organization also sponsored annual conferences on charity work, which brought
the leaders of the various independent charities together to discuss common problems and to hear prominent reformers such as Jacob Riis, the
author of the popular book concerning New York's slums entitled *How the
Other Half Lives,* who spoke several times on the problem of urban poverty.[72]

The Associated Charities offered a much more comprehensive approach
to welfare than Wilmington had ever known before. It proved to be the
most important but hardly the sole innovation in local philanthropy in the
latter years of the nineteenth century. During these same years both a
YMCA and a YWCA were launched, which developed varied athletic and
social programs as well as providing young working people with inexpensive but respectable housing. Independent philanthropists founded a reform school for boys, a society to care for unwed mothers, and homes for
both elderly blacks and aged white couples. On the east side Sarah Webb
Pyle, a young woman, inspired by the preaching of the evangelist Dwight
Moody, began a settlement house where she ran a kindergarten and offered instruction in practical and creative subjects such as gardening, sewing, and music.[73] Among the settlement's most popular activities were its
clubs for boys and girls, precursors of the scouting movement.

A most important series of philanthropic endeavors led to the creation
of two permanent hospitals in Wilmington. The wives of the city's indus-

[71] Emalea P. Warner, *The First Fifty Years,* pamphlet in possession of The Family Society,
pp. 8–9.
[72] *Annual Report, Associated Charities,* 1895, p. 20.
[73] *Sunday Star,* Jan. 20, 1918.

Wilmington, Delaware

66. *The Delaware Hospital* was built in 1888 at Fourteenth and Washington streets. (Courtesy H.S.D.)

trial and commercial leaders played a major role in the early days of these institutions just as they did in the Associated Charities. After the scandal associated with the city council's hospital in the 1870s, there was little enthusiasm for hospitals, but the need for a place where injured workmen could receive suitable care remained. In 1887 when Mrs. Mary H. Harrington, the daughter of a state judge and wife of a prominent lawyer and one-time mayor of the city, began raising funds for a free private hospital, many citizens were prepared to contribute. Mary Harrington's campaign floundered over the question of whether the proposed hospital was to follow the allopathic or homeopathic school of medicine. At this point Mrs. J. T. Gause, a devotee of homeopathy, induced her husband to purchase a large building and opened a hospital where the city's homeopaths might practice. The majority of the local physicians were allopaths, however, and after a brief respite, Mrs. Harrington's efforts were resumed and culminated in the establishment of the Delaware Hospital in 1888.[74] At first both hospitals had trouble filling their beds because prospective patients thought

[74] Charles A. Silliman, *The Hospital* (Wilmington, Del., 1966), pp. 6–14.

144

of them as extensions of the stigmatized almshouse, but by the mid-1890s this prejudice vanished. In 1893 the Delaware Hospital opened a free dispensary that was popular among the city's poor families.[75]

The hospitals adopted an administrative system similar to that of the Associated Charities. Each had an all-male board of trustees representing the major donors that supplied general supervision of finances, but most policy decisions were made by an all-female board of managers, many of whom were wives of trustees. Day-to-day operations were in the hands of a salaried employee: at the Associated Charities, a supervisor; in the hospital, the head nurse.

The desire on the part of wealthy women to participate more fully in activities outside the home culminated in the establishment of a women's club in Wilmington in 1889. Called the New Century Club, its purposes were a blend of the intellectual, social, and charitable impulses of the young matrons who organized it. The membership roster read like a *Who's Who* of Wilmington's leading professional and manufacturing families. The major figure in the club's early history and paradigm of the life-style the club-women aspired to was Mrs. Emalea Warner who lectured her fellow members on the new concept of femininity that she herself exemplified, "woman is a modern discovery; she herself, the discoverer . . . she has discovered that the same all-pervading influence and presence which exalts and purifies her home life she must take to the open door, nay further, step into the world. . . ."[76] In his study of American feminism, *Everyone Was Brave*, William O'Neill noted that the women's clubs were the least militant form of association for the "New Woman,"[77] since by accepting the traditional spheres of womanly endeavors—namely, culture and philanthropy—they avoided the strident militancy that appealed to relatively few women. Wilmington furnished thin soil for radical feminism; efforts to establish a suffragist group in the city in 1869 came to nought.[78] But where radicalism failed to take hold, the more moderate approach to improving society offered by the New Century Club proved to be very attractive to upper-middle-class women.

[75] *Ibid.*, p. 21.
[76] *Annual Report of the New Century Club* (Wilmington, Del., 1891), p. 2.
[77] William L. O'Neill, *Everyone Was Brave* (Chicago, 1969), pp. 103–4.
[78] *Wilmington Daily Commercial*, Nov. 20, 1869.

Wilmington, Delaware   The New Century Club's three hundred members represented the forces of both the exclusiveness and integration in fin de siècle Wilmington. Membership in New Century was limited to those in the group Canby described as "Us," but the club was concerned with political and social problems that gave it considerable scope. As an elitist group, the club drew Wilmington's prestigious families into a more closely knit unit. The club was the site of many entertainments for members and their families that narrowed the social distance that had formerly separated Quakers from other well-to-do Wilmingtonians. The clubwomen concerned themselves with the problems of their less affluent sisters, but they did not invite them to join the club.

The club aimed to raise the intellectual level of its members and to introduce more opportunities for cultural growth to all Wilmingtonians. New Century sponsored concerts and lecture series on art, literature, and current affairs. Professor Woodrow Wilson of Princeton, who visited the club whenever he came to Wilmington to consult with the local artist Howard Pyle, illustrator of his volumes on American history, was a favorite speaker. The club eagerly supported the idea of college and professional education for women. It held teas for local college girls to discuss their experiences with other prospective female students and offered lectures on the subject of female higher education. Mrs. Warner and other club members campaigned successfully to introduce a woman's college at the state university in Newark, fifteen miles from Wilmington. The club's philosophy was that no conflict need exist between a woman's family responsibilities and her professional aspirations, and the members took pride in the fact that a woman architect designed their clubhouse on Delaware Avenue.

It was in the realm of philanthropy and political reform, however, that the New Century Club really made itself a social force in Wilmington. As O'Neill points out, clubwomen throughout America had no direct political power since they could not vote, but the politicians could hardly ignore them because of the power their husbands wielded. The ladies were most active in the areas of educational and penal reform and in support of city charter reform. Their tactics were simple and straightforward. When the club had adopted some reform goal, members would invite public officials and local opinion leaders to attend a lecture and discussion session on the subject. If necessary, the club would follow up their initial appeal with more publicity and direct lobbying in Dover. Through these tactics the club, sometimes in conjunction with the Associated Charities that included many of the same members, was responsible for numerous reforms, including the public school lunch program, the erection of a modern county workhouse, the introduction of manual education in the public high schools, a compulsory school law, and laws to protect child and female factory workers. The club founded the state's first reform school for girls and, together with the Associated Charities, sponsored many conferences on social work where Wilmingtonians had an opportunity to hear leading social thinkers of the day.[79]

The Flowering of Organized Sports and Amusements

The relationship between lady-bountiful-style philanthropy and team sports and other entertainments is less obscure than it may appear to be at first glance. The same second generation that was responsible for the one was a major factor in the introduction of the other. The city's first choral societies, operetta groups, and even its first baseball team were all created by the children of those men whose affluence came from the city's industrial progress. That is not to say that other groups in the society—immigrants, middle-class and working-class people—were not important participants in the new forms of entertainment, but the wealthier citizens were often the catalysts in the introduction of both cultural and athletic activities. Ultimately, however, the introduction of such institutions as amusement parks, vaudeville theaters and sports teams depended upon urbanization and the coming of age of a new urban culture.

Before 1871 when the Masons, led by George G. Lobdell, president of the Lobdell Car Wheel Company, built an opera house with a seating capacity of twelve hundred on Market Street that attracted professional entertainers to the city, Wilmington had been a dull town, especially during the winter months.[80] Although the opera house proved to be a moderate success, the

---

[79] *Ibid.,* 1889–1900.
[80] *Wilmington Daily Commercial,* Nov. 1, 1866; July 20, 1870; Apr. 20, 1871.

67. *Masonic Temple and Grand Opera.* Built in 1871 on the east side of Market Street between Eighth and Ninth streets. The temple is an iron-front building designed by the architect Thomas Dixon, a native Wilmingtonian who practiced in Baltimore. (Courtesy H.S.D.)

high-minded *Every Evening* complained of Wilmingtonians' indiscriminate taste, which preferred minstrel shows with "stale jokes and flat music" to good plays.[81] The value of the theater went beyond this kind of criticism, however, because it did help to form taste, and more importantly, it brought Wilmington into the main stream of political and cultural events of national significance. Local theaters in the late nineteenth century functioned as molders of a mass society in much the same way as radio and television have done more recently. Henry George, William Jennings Bryan, and other spokesmen for controversial causes addressed overflowing crowds from the opera house stage, and leading actors and actresses performed the most popular plays of the day there. The opera house also encouraged local talent and brought the community together to see and hear their neighbors perform Gilbert and Sullivan operettas and choral works. The best among these local choral groups was the Tuesday Club, a collection of young people of both sexes "from the higher circles of society in the city,"[82] the Philharmonic Society, and the Delaware *Sängerbund,* a German-American society dedicated to the study and performance of music written by German composers.[83]

Other innovations in community life revolved around the introduction of organized sports. Prior to the 1860s, popular sports such as hunting, boating, and ice skating required very little cooperation among individuals. Baseball, introduced into Wilmington in 1865, demanded organization. In its early days in Wilmington, baseball was a gentleman's game played by those who could afford the time during daylight hours required for practice, as well as the considerable expense involved in buying a uniform and other gear. Wilmington's first team, the Diamond States, was recruited from young businessmen and the sons of industrialists and professional men. Dressed in black-and-white-check shirts, black pants with blue side stripes, blue belts, and topped by matching blue skull caps, each with a diamond on top, the proud players captured the interest of all who saw them. In their first game against the Philadelphia Athletics, one of the leading teams of the nation, the Diamond States lost by the whopping margin

[81] *Every Evening,* Jan. 21, 1876.
[82] Scharf, *History of Delaware,* 2:839.
[83] *Ibid.,* p. 838.

of 104 to 5, but their appearance spurred imitators.[84] Soon there was another local team, the Wawasets, who were more evenly matched against the Diamond States. In the late 1860s, baseball achieved the proportions of a mania in Wilmington, as it did elsewhere in the United States, and the games attracted large crowds of both male and female fans. As competition increased, the rival teams hired tough working-class boys who could bat, field, and pitch better than the amateurs they replaced.[85] Thus, its very popularity helped to make baseball a sport for professional as well as amateur players of all social classes. It would be difficult to overestimate the importance of baseball for urban America in the last years of the nineteenth century. It not only replaced the competition encouraged by the transportation boom as the major source of community solidarity against rival cities; the game also served as a common meeting ground for people from every social class.

Other sporting activities, including gymnastics, roller skating, bicycling, tennis, horse racing, golf, and football, also came into prominence at this time, largely through the efforts of several athletic clubs. German immigrants founded a *Turnverein* that specialized in body-building gymnastics.[86] Another group, called the Warren Athletic Club, that engaged in both indoor and outdoor sporting events, had attracted eight hundred members by 1892 when it first admitted females.[87] The so-called social set sponsored the Delaware Field Club, which offered its male members the chance to participate in tennis, cricket, baseball, and football, as well as tennis for the ladies.[88] In 1901 the club leased land from William du Pont just west of the city on which they laid out Wilmington's first golf course and built an imposing clubhouse. The field club then reorganized into a new, broader-based association called the Wilmington Country Club and began its career as a leading gathering spot for the city's social elite.[89]

At the turn of the century, sports were introduced into the city's high

---

[84] *Every Evening*, Aug. 17, 1887.
[85] *Ibid.*
[86] Abeles, "The German Element in Wilmington," p. 65.
[87] *Every Evening*, Apr. 19, 1892.
[88] *Ibid.*, Apr. 5, 1888.
[89] *Ibid.*, Apr. 2, 1901.

68. *A Trolley Car for Parties,* built in 1896 by Jackson & Sharp for the Wilmington City Railway Company to be rented to party-givers. The railway also had a funeral car for rent. (Courtesy E.M.H.L.)

schools. The Wilmington High School athletic program grew out of an athletic association started by the students in the 1890s. The school athletic contests gained popularity throughout the community and gave high school an aura of glamour that it had heretofore utterly lacked. Sports and other extracurricular activities such as drama and music societies made the school a focal point of community interest and attendance more appealing than in the past. School officials, however, soon discovered that sports were a mixed blessing, for although the chance to play on the high school teams

69. *The Trolley to the Park, ca. 1912*. Complete with brass band, this trolley car is about to leave Eighth and Market streets for Brandywine Springs Park. (Courtesy H.S.D.)

kept boys in school who would otherwise have dropped out, some students were neglecting their lessons in order to play. The principal at Wilmington High, therefore, urged the board of education to appoint an athletic director to the school staff who could control the number of games played and prevent students in poor standing from participating.[90] In 1906 Miss Kruse,

[90] *Annual Report of the Board of Education* (Wilmington, Del., 1903), p. 39.

the principal at Howard High School, reported a similar phenomenon. "For the past two or three years," she said, "there has been a growing interest in athletics in the school. With the formation of various kinds of athletic teams there has been noticeable a stronger desire on the part of the boys to conform to the standard of scholarship and an increased love for their school."[91]

Opportunities for leisure activities grew apace as the city expanded and as more people had the time and money for entertainment. Excursion boats operated each summer between Wilmington and various bay and ocean resorts. Several circuses, complete with parades to entice customers, visited town regularly. Most important of all were the amusement parks with their lakes for rowing and swimming, bandstands, live and marionette shows, dance halls, and exciting rides. Wilmington boasted three such pleasure gardens. Two, the Brandywine Springs Park and Shellpot Park, were developed by rival electric trolley companies in the 1890s as a means of increasing summer patronage. Located at their respective ends of the line, the parks maintained a lively competition by continually adding new attractions. The Brandywine Springs Park drew thirteen thousand customers on its opening day in 1901.[92] Wilmington's third amusement park, at Gordon Heights along the Delaware River, was the creation of a steamboat company. These parks were a central feature in the lives of working-class and middle-class families at the turn of the century.

The increasing level of organization and commercialization that had come to characterize the city's social life and amusements by the 1890s produced complex, even contradictory results. In one way these trends heightened class exclusiveness. The membership policies of the New Century Club and the Wilmington Country Club limited access to the city's "best" social circles as never before. Simultaneously, these same second-generation industrialist families were reaching out beyond Wilmington for inclusion in a wider circle of American upper-middle-class society by such means as involvement in the national conferences of women's clubs, sending their sons and daughters to prestigious colleges, and by taking vacation cruises to Europe.[93] But although this set of trends cut Wilmington society horizon-

[91] *Ibid.*, 1906, p. 53.   [92] Weslager, *Brandywine Springs*, p. 83.
[93] For a journalistic expression of the upper-class social scene at the turn of the century, see *Delaware Life*, a weekly magazine published in Wilmington, 1902–1903, H.S.D.

70 & 71. *Restaurant and Lake Front at Brandywine Springs Park* from *Souvenir of the Peoples Railway Co.* (Courtesy W.I.F.L.)

tally, another and more important impact of the new styles in urban entertainment and social life drew the city's people together by providing them with common experiences and loyalties. Relative to the experiences of the generation that had preceded them, the groups gaining the most from the amusement parks, vaudeville houses, and baseball teams were the working and middle classes. One wonders, for example, how important these increased leisure-time opportunities may have been in regard to the reduction of juvenile crime, but, unfortunately, the crime statistics of the Wilmington police in that period are too inadequate to attempt a comparison.

Wilmington may have been a sluggish city culturally, as its journalists claimed, and the city undoubtedly harbored many unresolved social problems, but it was no urban jungle; its people were not isolated from one another. A number of the reasons why the city was able to remain tranquil through a period of physical expansion and population growth had to do with its unique qualities: its relatively small size and moderate rate of growth, its varied industries drawing on skilled workmen and owned and managed by local men, the absence of suburbanization, its relatively low proportion of new Americans, and peaceful race relations. Other important factors, however, were common threads in American urbanization. The appearance of highly organized professional and amateur team and individual sports, the spread of vaudeville, and the popularity of amusement parks and fraternal lodges were ubiquitous elements in turn-of-the-century American culture. Their importance in making cities livable should not be overlooked.

72. *Building on a New Scale: The Du Pont Building and the Old New Castle County Court House, ca. 1910.* The court house was constructed in 1881 and demolished following World War I to make way for Rodney Square. The first section of the Du Pont Building was built in 1906. (Courtesy E.M.H.L.)

Epilogue

The first decade of the twentieth century marked as distinct a watershed in Wilmington's history as had the decade of the 1840s. In the years following 1900, the city's economic function was transformed from a center for heavy industry into its current image as "the chemical capital of the world," the home office of several internationally known chemical companies, Du Pont, Atlas, and Hercules.

Roots of the transformation lay in the decline of the older local industries as well as in the startling rise in fortunes of the du Ponts. Already in the 1890s Wilmington's rate of growth had begun to decline,[1] and between 1900 and 1910 the city's total industrial work force increased by only 240 individuals.[2]

There were various causes for the decline. The depression of the 1890s was surely a setback, yet other satellite industrial cities in the Philadelphia region of approximately Wilmington's size enjoyed a more rapid growth rate. Between 1899 and 1909, while Wilmington's force of industrial wage earners increased by a mere 1.1 percent, Trenton, New Jersey's grew by 41.1 percent, Reading, Pennsylvania's by 42.9 percent, and Camden, New Jersey's by 113.5 percent.[3]

U.S. census reports show only the quantifiable aspects of what was becoming a serious economic problem for the city, the decline of Wilmington's car- and shipbuilding trades and related industries. The reasons for the decline were largely beyond the control of local manufacturers. At the turn of the century, shifts in market demands and technological advances, together with the concentration of vast capital resources in the control of a few New York-based commercial banks, led to the creation of innumerable industrial combinations, or trusts as they were popularly called. The steel industry, closely related to car and ship construction, was particularly affected when the organizational skills of banker J. P. Morgan were added

[1] U.S. Census, 1910, *Population,* 2:268.
[2] U.S. Census, 1910, *Manufactures,* 8:94.
[3] *Ibid.,* p. 84.

to those of Andrew Carnegie to form the U.S. Steel Corporation. During these same years various important Wilmington car- and shipbuilding firms faced troubled times. The market for railroad cars declined as the nation's railroads reached a stage of completion, while Wilmington shipbuilders discovered that they lacked the equipment or capitalization to compete with the New York Ship Company's large modern plant built in 1899 at Camden, New Jersey. The leading executives of Wilmington's largest firms, Job Jackson and J. T. Gause, died within a year of one another in 1901, leaving to younger men in their respective companies the problems of competing under unfamiliar and unfavorable market conditions.

Each company suffered from problems peculiar to itself. Harlan & Hollingsworth broke a long-held company policy during the Spanish-American War period when it agreed to build a warship for the U.S. Navy. Harlan's had traditionally refused Navy contracts because of the close supervision and regulatory standards imposed on government projects. The shipyard built a torpedo boat, the U.S.S. *Stringham*, which proved to be a costly mistake for the firm. The ship failed to reach its specified speed and suffered a broken propeller shaft shortly after it was commissioned.[4] In 1899, while its executives worried about increases in steel prices, Harlan's was struck by its machinists and painters. It is difficult to know which in this series of demoralizing events figured most in the management's decision to sell out to J. P. Morgan's U.S. Ship Company, a newly formed trust affiliated with U.S. Steel Corporation, in 1902. When the shipping trust proved to be unworkable, Harlan's was acquired by Charles Schwab's Bethlehem Steel Corporation. Just one in a series of trust-owned shipyards—the Harlan plant, as Bethlehem called it—was used only when it offered comparative advantages over others under Schwab's control. Henceforth, improvements designed to make the plant more competitive could only be made at the behest of out-of-town executives who were not concerned with the possible effects of their decisions on Wilmington's economy. Pusey & Jones, Wilmington's other major shipbuilding firm, was saved from a similar fate only because the firm's paper machinery business was strong enough to prompt Wilmington bankers to save the company.[5]

[4] David B. Tyler, *The American Clyde* (Newark, Del., 1958), p. 88.
[5] *Every Evening*, May 9, 1903, and Thomas Savery Papers, accession no. 489, John D. Kurtz Report on Condition of Pusey & Jones Company, June 1903, E.M.H.L.

Meanwhile, the city's carbuilding businesses were similarly depressed. Upon Job Jackson's death, the management of Jackson & Sharp decided to sell out to American Car and Foundry, a St. Louis-based combine. The Lobdell Car Wheel Company, already pressured by the narrowing sales market, successfully fought a suit by which it would have been forced to join with the trust in its field, the National Car Wheel Company.[6] But the legal victory did little to save the company from its own outmoded technology, epitomized by Lobdell's reluctance to abandon the chilled iron wheel in favor of steel.

Wilmington's industrialists, real estate men and retail merchants, could see the change coming over the city, and they worried about Wilmington's future in an era of giant trusts dominated by men sitting in New York board rooms. The board of trade, neglected since the days of Joshua T. Heald, was revived at the turn of the century in the hope that by a cooperative public relations campaign, Wilmington's businessmen could do something about the problem. For several years the board published a monthly journal that aimed at keeping local businessmen informed about their city and to make Wilmington attractive to outside investors. Concurrently, the board established a company that was to publicize the city's advantages as an industrial site through direct contacts with companies known to be seeking factory locations. Neither of these approaches proved to be very fruitful. After several years of solicitations, the industrial development company could boast of only a few successes, mostly in bringing knitting mills to the city. In spite of the board's efforts, the total number of manufacturing establishments in the city declined from 262 to 247, and the number of wage earners dropped from 14,498 to 13,554 in the first five years of the new century.[7]

Ironically, while the board of trade centered its attention on the manufacturing sector of the economy, the city's future was unfolding in another direction altogether. In 1902 Eugene du Pont, president of the Du Pont Powder Company, the largest American producer of gunpowder, died. The company, located on the Brandywine a few miles north of the city, had a long, if heretofore tangential, association with it. The president's death signaled a crisis in the company management out of which emerged

[6] *Every Evening*, Aug. 2, 1904.
[7] *Ibid.*, Nov. 23, 1906.

the aggressive leadership of three young and ambitious cousins, T. Coleman du Pont, Pierre S. du Pont, and Alfred I. du Pont. The cousins, attuned to the dynamics and demands of the new style of business operations, were eager to expand the company's control over the explosives industry and to move into related fields in chemistry. To do this, they needed a large, centralized office staff. In a move that was to have a momentous effect on Wilmington's subsequent development, they decided to make the city the headquarters of their enterprise. In 1906 they announced plans to build a twelve-story office building at Tenth and Market streets.[8] Interestingly enough, this decision was ignored by the board of trade despite the fact that the du Ponts would employ about 2,500 workers in their new building. Construction was quickly gotten under way, and the first stage of the Du Pont Building was completed in 1907. In the next few years the company built two large additions, including a theater and a first-class hotel. Two new powder companies, Atlas and Hercules, formed as a result of a federal antitrust suit against Du Pont, also located their administrative offices in the city, thus aiding the transformation. By 1914, Wilmington the industrial city had given way to a city of corporate management.

The land use patterns and social forms that had evolved in Wilmington under the impact of industrialization were swept away by further economic change. The shift of Wilmington's economic center from the factories along the Christina to uptown office buildings was only one in a series of changes that have shaped twentieth-century Wilmington, including the introduction of the automobile, black migration from the South, and the decline of European immigration. The old predominently blue-collar industrial city with its indigenous upper-middle-class leadership was replaced by a city of white-collar workers, many of whom chose to live in the suburbs. The economic leaders who made the major decisions affecting Wilmington continued to live nearby, if not in the city itself, and to take pride in local civic progress, but in the twentieth century the concentration of wealth and power among the city's major businessmen was far greater than in the past. Job Jackson and J. T. Gause never commanded anything approaching the potential power of P. S. du Pont. Especially following their company's spectacular profits in World War I, the du Pont family occupied a posi-

[8] *Ibid.*, Jan. 16, 1906.

160

tion apart from other Wilmingtonians of even the upper-middle-class as no family or individual had been in the nineteenth century.

Wilmington the corporation city is a very different place from its nineteenth-century predecessor. The remains of the old city, mostly in the form of factories abandoned or converted into warehouses and of decaying rows of brick homes that now house the largely black midtown urban population have prompted massive urban renewal projects designed to revitalize the older parts of the city economically and socially. But the heritage from the past is much more than these old buildings and the now outmoded economy they were constructed to serve. It is the spirit of cooperation that made nineteenth-century Wilmington into a livable industrial city.

Appendix
Bibliography
Index

Appendix

Tables 1 and 2

U.S. census reports reveal the evolution of Wilmington's major industries and the decline of those trades that shifted to larger urban regions in the wake of the revolutions in both manufacturing and transportation technologies. Table 1 represents Wilmington's ten leading industries based on annual value of product in three census years, 1860, 1880, and 1900. The latter two represent Wilmington alone, whereas the 1860 figures include all of New Castle County. This difference accounts for the higher value attached to the cotton and paper industries in the earliest year, since many factories engaged in these industries were located near, but outside, the city. Table 2 shows the ten leading industries in terms of work force. Note that the 1860 census lists car wheels separately, while in 1880 and 1900 they are included in foundry work.

Census statistics demonstrate that several of the industries that had been established in Wilmington in the early days of railroading continued to predominate as late as 1900. Between 1860 and 1900 flour milling, cotton textiles, carriage making and shipbuilding declined in importance, but all except flour remained among the city's leading trades. The published census did not include statistics on the makeup of the work force prior to 1880, but after that date it becomes possible to trace changes in the types of jobs that existed in Wilmington's economy. The percentage of the total city work force engaged in manufactures changed little during the years from 1880 to 1910. In 1880, 44.4 percent of Wilmington's workers were employed in manufactures; in 1900, 46.2 percent; the peak year was 1910 when 51 percent of the city's workers were in manufactures. By 1920 the percentage declined slightly to 48.7 percent. The rise of service trades, which Warner discovered was characteristic of Philadelphia's economy in the early twentieth century was very gradual in this manufacture-oriented city.[1] The percentage of the work force engaged in white-collar activities rose from 10.2 percent in 1880 to 16.6 percent in 1900 and 17 percent by 1910. The percentage of people employed by manufacturers in salaried positions rose from 7 percent of the industrial work force in 1890 to 12 percent by 1910.[2]

[1] Sam B. Warner, "A Scaffolding for Urban History," *American Historical Review* 74 (1968): 32.

[2] U.S. Census, 1880, *Population*, 1:908, *Statistics of Manufacturers*, 2:206; 1890, *Population*, 2:740–41, *Report on Manufacturing Industries*, 2:620–21; 1900, *Manufactures*, 2:112–13, *Occupations*, 8:758–61; 1910, *Population*, 4:287–90, *Manufactures*, 9:180–81; 1920, *Population*, 3:1248–49, 4:222–39.

Table 1. Ten leading industries, in annual value of products

	1860		1880		1900	
1	Flour	$1,537,266	Iron & steel	$2,004,570	Leather	$9,379,504
2	Cotton goods	941,703	Shipbuilding	1,974,203	Cars	3,540,144
3	Leather	894,980	Leather	1,801,597	Foundry & machine	3,299,509
4	Shipbuilding	574,650	Cars	1,185,688	Iron & steel	2,934,993
5	Car wheels	562,000	Paper & printing	682,905	Carpentering	694,735
6	Carriages	553,250	Foundry & machine	671,125	Beer	614,896
7	Paper & printing	385,000	Cotton goods	545,460	Bread	452,843
8	Machines	348,500	Carriages	479,067	Plumbing	422,608
9	Iron manufacture	341,953	Carpentering	202,200	Meatpacking	415,144
10	Boot & shoe	196,241	Tin & sheet iron	159,027	Pulp goods	301,018

Table 2. Ten leading industries, by number of workers

	1860		1880		1900	
1	Cotton goods	1,109	Shipbuilding	1,454	Cars	2,897
2	Shipbuilding	558	Leather	914	Leather	2,454
3	Carriages	523	Cars	860	Foundry & machine	2,009
4	Leather	384	Foundry & machine	779	Iron & steel	1,327
5	Machines	325	Iron & steel	610	Hosiery & knitting	470
6	Boot and shoe	307	Cotton goods	469	Carpentering	199
7	Car wheels	200	Carriages	384	Bakery	180
8	Iron	193	Brickmaking	234	Carriages	176
9	Cooperage	170	Paper & printing	230	Shipbuilding	176
10	Cars	100	Carpentering	105	Printing	162

SOURCES: U.S. Census, 1860, *Manufactures*, 53–54; U.S. Census, 1880, *Statistics of Manufactures*, 2:444–45; U.S. Census, 1900, *Manufactures*, 8:112–13.

Table 3

One of Wilmington's major attractions for industry in the nineteenth century was the availability of cheap skilled labor. The Wilmington board of trade claimed that their city offered a substantially lower cost of living, particularly for housing, than did Philadelphia and other larger eastern industrial centers. As a corollary, Wilmington's boosters argued that a large percentage of Wilmington's workingmen were homeowners and were therefore more settled and contented than their bretheren in other cities.

The evidence available to historians only partially substantiates the claim that Wilmington's working class were docile homeowners. In regard to the cost of housing in Philadelphia and Wilmington, it would appear that working-class housing was less expensive in the smaller city, although the gap narrowed toward the end of the century. In 1871 when new two-story row houses in Wilmington were selling for approximately $1,500, comparable houses were selling for twice as much in Philadelphia. In the early 1880s six-room houses in Wilmington's east-side working-class district rented for between thirteen and fifteen dollars, whereas rent in Philadelphia for the same-sized house was about twenty dollars.[1]

In 1900 the U.S. census for the first time reported figures on the number of homes that were rented, mortgaged, or free of debt. These tables provide a reasonably accurate measure of the claim that homeownership was more common in Wilmington than in other industrial cities. Table 3 below shows that 69 percent of the homes in Wilmington were rented and that the percentage of renters versus owners varied very little throughout the city. This figure was not appreciably different from such nearby industrial cities as Philadelphia where 74 percent of the houses were rented; Trenton, New Jersey, where 71 percent were rented; Chester, Pennsylvania, 71.8 percent; and Camden, New Jersey, 71.6 percent.[2]

[1] Hoffecker, "Nineteenth Century Wilmington . . . ," *Delaware History* 15 (1972), 14.
[2] U.S. Census, 1900, *Population,* 2:704–9.

Table 3. Homeownership, by wards

Ward	Free	Encumbered	Rented	Total
1	43	37	291	540
2	96	84	877	1,092
3	112	104	744	1,020
4	80	61	558	751
5	278	348	1,137	1,894
6	124	145	885	1,243
7	394	499	1,611	2,583
8	161	205	1,394	1,867
9	100	253	1,030	1,456
10	142	217	918	1,325
11	78	102	511	731
12	53	154	674	908
Total	1,661	2,209	10,630	15,410
% of Total	11%	14%	69%	

Source: U.S. Census, 1900, *Population,* 2:702.

Bibliography

The most useful collections of both primary and secondary materials relevant to the history of Wilmington are to be found in the Wilmington Institute Free Library (W.I.F.L.), the Historical Society of Delaware (H.S.D.), the Archives of the State of Delaware (A.S.D.), the Hugh M. Morris Library of the University of Delaware (H.M.M.L.), and the Eleutherian Mills Historical Library (E.M.H.L.). By far the largest number of the works listed below came from one of these collections. The archives of churches and social agencies and private interviews provided additional resources. The bibliography that follows includes only those works which provided useful insights into life in nineteenth-century Wilmington.

Primary Sources

MANUSCRIPTS

Bancroft-Bird Collection. H.S.D.

Bethlehem Shipbuilding Corporation. List of ships built at the Harlan Plant. Acc. 277, E.M.H.L.

Board of Trustees. Grace Methodist-Episcopal Church. Minute book, 1864–1867. In possession of the church.

Bush, George W., Reminiscences. Snader Collection, H.S.D.

Delaware Association for the Moral Improvement and Education of the Colored People, Address, 1866. H.S.D.

Delaware Association for the Moral Improvement and Education of the Colored People. Minute book, 1866–1876. H.S.D.

Delaware Senate Journal, 1831–1832. A.S.D.

Eden Lodge #34 I.O.O.F. Assorted papers and membership lists. In possession of the lodge.

Exposition of the state of pauperism and of the state of the finances, receipts, and expenditures for the poor of New Castle County for the year 1826. H.S.D.

Bibliography   Family Society of Wilmington, Delaware. Assorted papers, minute book and annual reports, 1886–1912, of the Associated Charities. In possession of the society.

"History of the Wilmington and Northern Railroad. Obtained from files of Mr. George Rommel, Master Mechanic." Typewritten manuscript. W.I.F.L.

Home for Destitute and Friendless Children. Minutes and annual reports, 1864–1912. H.M.M.L.

Journal of the Proceedings of the Diocesan Convention of Delaware, 1843–1909. Office of the Episcopal Diocese of Delaware.

Massey, George V., II. "Of Gold, Ships and Sand: The History of the Warner Company, 1794–1929." Edited by Norman Wilkinson and Harold Hancock. Microfilm copy. E.M.H.L.

McLear and Kendall Company. Correspondence with Francis G. du Pont. Acc. 504, E.M.H.L.

The National Council of the Order of United American Mechanics. Minute book, 1856–1872. Acc. 307, E.M.H.L.

Nelson, Alice D. "Big Quarterly in Wilmington." Typewritten in 1932. W.I.F.L.

Pusey, Charles W. "A Brief History of the Pusey and Jones Company." Typewritten and dated May 23, 1921. Acc. 369, E.M.H.L.

Pusey & Jones Company. Copy of an apprenticeship agreement between the company and John E. Whitehead. Dated April 30, 1877. Acc. 369, E.M.H.L.

"Rules for Workers of Bush and Lobdell Company, 1841." Photostatic copy. Acc. 608, E.M.H.L.

Savery, Thomas H. Correspondence, diary, and other material. Accs. 291, 489, and 915, E.M.H.L.

"Welfare Work at the Plant of Joseph Bancroft and Sons Company." Typewritten report, 1912. Acc. 940, E.M.H.L.

West End Neighborhood House. Minute book, 1913–1916, and other files. In possession of the house.

Wilmington Board of Trade. Minute book, Sept. 1867–Sept. 1875. Acc. 1016, E.M.H.L.

Wilmington and Brandywine Railroad Reports Relating to Surveys, 1860. W.I.F.L.

NEWSPAPERS

Blue Hen's Chicken (Wilmington, Del.), 1849.

Delaware Free Press (Wilmington, Del.), 1830–1832.

Delaware Gazette (Wilmington, Del.), 1861.

Delaware Gazette and American Watchman (Wilmington, Del.), 1833–1847.

Delaware Journal and Statesman (Wilmington, Del.), 1862.

Delaware State Journal (Wilmington, Del.), 1855–1859, 1862–1865.

Every Evening (Wilmington, Del.), 1871–1910.

James and Webb's Holiday Visitor, Supplement (Wilmington, Del.), 1883–1884.

The Morning News (Wilmington, Del.), 1880–1900, scattered copies.

Niles Register (Baltimore, Md.), vol. IX, no. 6

Sunday Star (Wilmington, Del.), 1881–1910.

Wilmington Daily Commercial, 1866–1871.

The Wilmingtonian, 1885.

MAGAZINES

Delaware Life (Wilmington, Del.), 1902.

Harkness Magazine (Wilmington, Del.), 1872–1873.

Lippincott's Magazine (Philadelphia), April and May 1873.

Outlook (New York), June 10, 1911.

INTERVIEWS

Allmond, W. Stewart. Transcribed interview conducted by Faith Pizor and John Scafidi, June 10 and July 1, 1969. E.M.H.L.

Mullen, D. Ethelda. Conducted by the author, February 1969.

Rhoads, J. Edgar. Transcribed interview conducted by Faith Pizor, Norman Wilkinson, and Lucius Ellsworth, Janurary 31, 1969. E.M.H.L.

———. Conducted by the author, February 1970.

Stirlith, Frank T. Transcribed interview conducted by J. P. Monigle and Norman Wilkinson, January 12 and 14, 1960. E.M.H.L.

Ward, H. H. Conducted by the author, February 1969.

Young, Pauline. Conducted by the author, January 1969.

Bibliography   Maps

Atlas of the City of Wilmington, Delaware and Vicinity. Philadelphia: G. W. Baist, 1887.

Baist's Atlas, New Castle County. Philadelphia: G. W. Baist, 1893.

Baist's Property Atlas of the City of Wilmington, Delaware. Philadelphia: G. W. Baist, 1901.

City Atlas of Wilmington, Delaware. Philadelphia: G. M. Hopkins, 1876.

Hexamer's General Survey of Wilmington, Delaware. Philadelphia: Sanborn Map Company, 1866, 1876, 1884.

Plan of The City of Wilmington. Philadelphia: Richard Clark, 1850.

Plan of The City of Wilmington, G. R. Riddle, 1847. Photocopy, E.M.H.L.

Pomeroy and Beer's New Topographical Atlas of the State of Delaware. Philadelphia: Pomeroy & Beer, 1868.

Wilmington Map, 1804, unidentified source. Photocopy. E.M.H.L.

Secondary Sources

Pamphlets

Adas Kodesch Congregation. Golden Jubilee, 1890–1940.

Annual Report, Delaware Society for the Prevention of Cruelty to Children, 1896.

Annual Report, New Century Club, 1899–1913.

Annual Report, Wilmington Institute, 1862–1894.

Annual Report, Wilmington Institute Free Library, 1895–1912.

Association of Manufacturers of Chilled Car Wheels. Historical Sketch of the Lobdell Car Wheel Company, 1836–1936.

Bates, Hon. Daniel M. "Memorial Address on the Life and Character of Willard Hall," 1879. Historical and Biographical Papers, H.S.D., vol. I.

Bissell, Emily P. Historical Sketch of Rodney Street Sunday School, 1904. Board of Trade Journal, 1898–1906.

Bush, Charles W. History of the Y.M.C.A., Wilmington, Delaware, 1954.

Bush, Lewis P., M.D. "Life and Character of Benjamin Ferris," 1903. Historical and Biographical Papers, H.S.D., vol. IV.

————. *Some Vital Statistics of the City of Wilmington*, 1877.

Catalogue of Rugby Academy, 1876.

Contractors and Builders Handy Book of the Builders Exchange, 1892–93.

Dedication of the Wilmington High School Building, 1901.

Diamond State Telephone Company. *Wilmington, Old and New*, 1929.

The Discipline of the Union American Methodist-Episcopal Church, 1872.

The Executive Committee of the Alumni. *Biographical Catalogue of the Graduates of the Wilmington High School, 1875–1895.*

50th Anniversary of the Founding of the Pusey and Jones Company, Wilmington, Delaware, 1848–1898.

First and Central Presbyterian Church, 200th Anniversary, 1937.

Fraim, Robert C. *Freemasonry in Delaware from 1769 to 1889*, 1890.

Guide Book and Industrial Journal of the Philadelphia, Wilmington, and Baltimore Railroad, 1877.

Hall, Hon. Willard. *Report of the Annual School Convention of New Castle County*, Feb. 1849.

Haupt, Lewis M. *Report on the Harbor of Wilmington, Delaware, and the Improvement of the Christiana River*, 1888.

Hering, Rudolph. *Report on a System of Sewerage for the City of Wilmington, Delaware*, 1883.

A Historical Sketch of the Wilmington Library and Young Men's Association, 1858.

History of the Female Benevolent Society, n.d.

A History of the Wilmington Whist Club, 1891–1955.

The Homeopathic Hospital, 50th Anniversary, 1888–1938.

Isaacs, I. J., ed. *Commerce, Manufactures, and Resources of Wilmington, Delaware, and Environs.* Syracuse, N.Y., 1887.

Jackson & Sharp Company. *Catalogue*, 1894.

Jones, Theophilus K. "Recollections of Wilmington from 1845 to 1860," 1909. *Historical and Biographical Papers*, H.S.D., vol. V.

Lobdell Car Wheel Company, *Catalogue*, 1892.

Lore, Hon. Charles B. "Life and Character of Edward W. Gilpin," 1902. *Historical and Biographical Papers*, H.S.D., vol. IV.

————. "Memoir of Pennock Pusey," 1903. *Historical and Biographical Papers*, H.S.D., vol. IV.

Bibliography

Manual of the City Council, 1885–1886.

Maull, D. W., M.D. *A Municipal Hospital, A Necessity,* 1873.

Minquadale Home of Wilmington, Delaware. *Charter, By-Laws, Rules, and Regulations,* 1896.

Minutes of the Wilmington Annual Conference, Methodist-Episcopal Church, 1869–1880.

Mutual Audit Company of Louisville, Kentucky. *Financial Report Relating to the Investigation of the Water Department, City of Wilmington, 1883–1907,* 1907.

Organization of the United Companies Under the Name of the Philadelphia, Wilmington, and Baltimore Railroad Company, with Articles of Union and 2nd Annual Report, Philadelphia, 1838.

Pennewell, Hon. James. "The Life and Public Services of Hon. Charles B. Lore," 1913. *Historical and Biographical Papers,* H.S.D., vol. VII.

Pierson, Laura M. *YWCA, 1895–1945.*

Proceedings of the 25th Anniversary of the Organization of Grace Methodist-Episcopal Church, 1890.

Report of the Board of Managers of the Home for Aged Women, 1892.

Report of the Chief of Police, 1897–1915, including John B. Taylor, "Report on the Police Department in the City of Wilmington, Delaware: Analysis and Recommendations," 1914.

Report of the Commission Appointed to Consider the Question of Municipal Government So Far As It Relates to the City of Wilmington, 1897.

Report of the Committee Appointed by the City Council of Wilmington Relative to an Improvement of the City Water Works, 1849.

Report of a Committee of Citizens to the City Council on the Subject of a Public Park for the City of Wilmington, 1869.

A Report Concerning Conditions of Toilers in Delaware Together with a Supplementary Report on the Agricultural Industries, 1910, Episcopal Diocese of Delaware.

Report of the Delaware Association for the Moral Improvement and Education of the Colored People of the State, 1868.

Report of the Peoples Settlement Association, 1901–1913.

Sacred Heart R.C. Church. *Diamond Jubilee, 1874–1949.*

7th Annual Report of the Ladies of Charity of St. Vincent de Paul, 1908–1915.

174

A Statement of the Organization and Work of the Wilmington Fountain Society, n.d.

Thatcher, Albert Garrett. "Reminiscences, 1846–1928." Offprint from *The Spindle,* organ of the Standard-Coosa-Thatcher Company, 1924.

25th Annual Convention Report of the Delaware W.C.T.U., 1904.

250th Anniversary Year, J. E. Rhoads and Sons, 1952.

Vestry of St. Andrews P.E. Church. *Alfred Lee, First Bishop of Delaware,* 1888.

Warner, Emalea P. *The First Fifty Years, 1884–1934,* 1934.

West End Neighborhood House. *60 Years of Service, 1891–1951.*

Wilmington Association, United Building Trades, 1906.

The Wilmington Board of Trade Journal Illustrated Supplement, June 1900.

Wilmington Boarding School for Girls. *Catalogue,* 1845.

Wilmington, Delaware. *Annual Report, Board of Directors, Street and Sewer Department,* 1887–1901.

———. *Annual Report, Board of Education of the City of Wilmington,* 1872–1912.

———. *Annual Report, Board of Health of the City of Wilmington,* 1885–1914.

———. *Annual Report of the Board of Managers of the Wilmington Board of Trade,* 1867–1873, 1901–1903.

———. *Annual Report of the Board of Park Commissioners of Wilmington, Delaware,* 1895–1910.

———. *Annual Report of the Board of Public Utility Commissioners for the City of Wilmington,* 1912–1913.

———. *Annual Report of the Chief Engineer of the Water Department,* 1872, 1885, 1899, 1909–1910.

The Wilmington and Reading Rail Road Guide from Coal to Tide, 1870.

Wilmington Savings Fund Society. *One Hundred Years in Wilmington, 1832–1932.*

Worden, Victoria V. *A History of the Delaware State Board of Health,* n.d.

YMCA Yearbook, 1898–1906.

Zion Evangelical Lutheran Church. *Ninety Years in Zion, 1848–1938.*

UNPUBLISHED THESES

Abeles, J. Emil. "The German Element in Wilmington from 1850 to 1914." M.A. thesis, University of Delaware, 1948.

Bibliography   Artner, Gail Marie. "Priest and Parish in the Formative Years, 1800–1840." M.A. thesis, University of Delaware, 1968.

Dew, Thomas R. "Delaware's First Labor Party." M.A. thesis, University of Delaware, 1959.

Drescher, Nuala M. "The Irish in Industrial Wilmington, 1800–1845." M.A. thesis, University of Delaware, 1960.

Farris, Sally G. "The Wilmington Merchant, 1775–1815." M.A. thesis, University of Delaware, 1961.

Hiller, Amy M. "The Disfranchisement of the Delaware Negroes in the Late Nineteenth Century." M.A. thesis, University of Delaware, 1965.

Kcmpski, Leonard John. "A History of Catholicism in Delaware, 1704–1868." M.A. thesis, University of Delaware, 1965.

Kerr, William T. "Ideology and Urbanization, Business Response to Social Needs in Late-Nineteenth-Century Wilmington, Delaware." M.A. thesis, University of Delaware, 1964.

Lukaszewski, Chester P., Jr. "The Wilmington Volunteer Fire Department, 1775–1921." M.A. thesis, University of Delaware, 1965.

Potter, Jack C. "The Philadelphia, Wilmington, and Baltimore Railroad, 1831–1840: A Study in Early Railroad Transportation." M.A. thesis, University of Delaware, 1960.

Scafidi, Polly. "History of the Speakman Company." M.A. thesis, University of Delaware, 1968.

Touhey, Mother St. Philip, O.S.U. "A History of Catholic Education in the Diocese of Wilmington, Delaware." M.A. thesis, Catholic University of America, 1957.

ARTICLES

Bohner, Charles H. "Rum and Reform: Temperance in Delaware Politics." *Delaware History* 5 (1952–53): 237–69.

Bounds, Harvey. "Wilmington Match Companies." *Delaware History* 10 (1962–63): 3–32.

Calvert, Monte A. "The Wilmington Board of Trade, 1867–1875." *Delaware History* 12 (1966–67): 175–97.

Chance, Elbert. "The Great Days of Wilmington's Grand Opera House." *Delaware History* 8 (1958–59): 185–99.

Collins, W. H. "History of Bethlehem's Wilmington Plant." The Society of

176

Naval Architects and Marine Engineers, *Historical Transactions,* 1893–1943: 208–12.

Garvan, Anthony N.B. "Proprietary Philadelphia As Artifact." In *The Historian and the City.* Ed. Oscar Handlin and John Burchard, pp. 177–201. Cambridge: M.I.T. Press, 1963.

Gutman, Herbert G. "Class, Status, and Community Power in Nineteenth-Century American Industrial Cities—Paterson, New Jersey: A Case Study." In *The Age of Industrialism in America.* Ed. Frederic C. Jaher, pp. 263–87. New York: The Free Press, 1968.

Hancock, Harold B. "The Status of the Negro in Delaware After the Civil War, 1865–1875." *Delaware History* 13 (1968–69): 57–66.

Hoffecker, Carol E. "Church Gothic: A Case Study of Revival Architecture in Wilmington, Delaware." *Winterthur Portfolio* 8 (Fall 1972): 215–31.

———. "Nineteenth-Century Wilmington: Satellite or Independent City?" *Delaware History* 15 (1972–73): 1–18.

Lang, William L. "Francis Vincent and the *Blue Hen's Chicken.*" *Delaware History* 13 (1968–69): 28–45.

Lemon, James T. "Urbanization and the Development of Eighteenth-Century Southeastern Pennsylvania and Adjacent Delaware." *William and Mary Quarterly* 24 (1966–67): 501–42.

Livesay, Harold C. "Delaware Negroes, 1865–1915." *Delaware History* 13 (1968–69): 87–123.

———. "The Lobdell Car Wheel Company, 1830–1867." *Business History Review* 42 (1968): 171–94.

Peltier, David P. "Nineteenth-Century Voting Patterns in Delaware." *Delaware History* 13 (1968–69): 219–33.

Welsh, Peter C. "A Craft that Resisted Change: American Tanning Practices to 1850." *Technology and Culture* 4 (1963): 299–317.

———. "Merchants, Millers, and Ocean Ships: The Components of an Early American Industrial Town." *Delaware History* 7 (1956–57): 319–37.

BOOKS

Annual Report of the Secretary of Internal Affairs of the Commonwealth of Pennsylvania, part 3, "Industrial Statistics," 19. 1891.

Biographical and Genealogical History of the State of Delaware. 2 vols. Chambersburg, Pa.: J. M. Runk & Co., 1899.

Bibliography Bureau of Municipal Research. *Survey of the Government of the City of Wilmington, Delaware.* New York, 1919.

Bush, Charles W., et al. *Friends School in Wilmington.* Wilmington, Del., 1948.

Canby, Henry Seidel. *The Age of Confidence.* New York: Farrar & Rinehart, 1934.

Clark, Victor S. *History of Manufactures in the United States, 1607–1860.* Washington, D.C.: Carnegie Institution, 1916.

Clement, A. J. *Wilmington, Delaware, Its Productive Industries and Commercial and Maritime Advantages.* Wilmington, Del.: Wilmington Board of Trade, 1888.

Cole, Donald B. *Immigrant City.* Chapel Hill, N.C.: University of North Carolina Press, 1963.

Conrad, Henry C. *History of the State of Delaware.* 3 vols. Wilmington, Del., 1908.

Cook, Richard B. *The Early and Later Delaware Baptists.* Philadelphia: American Baptist Publication Society, 1880.

Cross, Robert D. *The Church and the City.* New York: Bobbs-Merrill Co., 1967.

Delaware's Industries. Philadelphia: Keighton Printing House, 1891.

Dexter, Seymour. *A Treatise on Co-operative Savings and Loan Associations.* New York: D. Appleton & Co., 1889.

Doherty, Robert W. *The Hicksite Separation.* New Brunswick, N.J.: Rutgers University Press, 1967.

Edwards, Richard, ed. *Industries of Delaware.* Wilmington, Del., 1880.

Every Evening, *History of Wilmington.* Wilmington, Del.: Every Evening Co., 1894.

Ferris, Benjamin. *A History of the Original Settlements on the Delaware.* Wilmington, Del.: Wilson & Heald, 1846.

Friends in Wilmington, 1738–1938. Wilmington, Del.: Charles L. Story, 1938.

Greeley, Horace, et al. *The Great Industries of the United States.* Hartford: J. B. Burr, Hyde & Co., 1872.

Green, Charles E. *History of the Grand Lodge of the A.F. and A.M. of Delaware.* Wilmington, Del.: Wm. N. Cann, 1956.

Grier, A. O. H. *This Was Wilmington.* Wilmington, Del.: News-Journal Co., 1945.

Hacker, Louis M. *The Triumph of American Capitalism.* New York: Simon & Schuster, 1940.

178

Hanna, John D. C., ed. *The Centennial Services of Asbury Methodist-Episcopal Church*. Wilmington, Del., 1889.

The Harlan and Hollingsworth Company, Ship and Car Builders, Their Plant and Operations. Philadelphia: Armstrong & Fears, 1898.

Henry, Allan J., ed. *The Life of Alexis Irénée du Pont*. 2 vols. Philadelphia: Wm. F. Fell Co., 1945.

Hilles, Samuel E. *Memorials of the Hilles Family*. Cincinnati, 1928.

Hutchins, John G. B. *The American Maritime Industries and Public Policy, 1789–1914*. Cambridge, Mass.: Harvard University Press, 1941.

Johnson, Allen, ed. *Dictionary of American Biography*. 23 vols. New York: Charles Scribner's Sons, 1928.

Katz, Michael B. *The Irony of Early School Reform: Educational Innovation in Mid-Nineteenth-Century Massachusetts*. Cambridge, Mass.: Harvard University Press, 1968.

Kenngott, George F. *The Record of a City*. New York: The Macmillan Co., 1912.

Kuhlmann, Charles B. *The Development of the Flour-Milling Industry in the United States*. Boston: Houghton Mifflin Co., 1929.

Lincoln, Anna T. *Wilmington, Delaware: Three Centuries Under Four Flags, 1609–1937*. Rutland, Vt.: Tuttle Publishing Co., 1937.

Livingood, James. *Philadelphia-Baltimore Trade Rivalry, 1780–1860*. Harrisburg, Pa.: Pennsylvania Historical and Museum Commission, 1947.

Lunt, Dudley. *The Wilmington Club, 1855–1955*. Wilmington, Del., 1955.

McCarter, J. M., and B. F. Jackson, eds. *Historical and Biographical Encyclopaedia of Delaware*. Wilmington, Del.: Aldine Printers, 1882.

Montgomery, Elizabeth. *Reminiscences of Wilmington*. Wilmington, Del., 1872.

O'Neill, William. *Everyone Was Brave*. Chicago: Quadrangle, 1969.

Ordinances and Acts of the General Assembly Relating to the City of Wilmington. Wilmington, Del., 1893.

Ordinances of the City of Wilmington, The. Wilmington, Del., 1841, 1849, 1857, 1859, 1863, 1866, 1869, 1893.

Powell, Lyman P. *The History of Education in Delaware*. Washington, D.C.: U.S.G.P.O., 1893.

Pred, Allen R. *The Spatial Dynamics of U.S. Urban-Industrial Growth, 1800–1914*. Cambridge, Mass.: Massachusetts Institute of Technology Press, 1966.

Reed, H. Clay, ed. *Delaware, A History of the First State*. 3 vols. New York: Lewis Historical Publishing Co., 1947.

————, ed. "Readings in Delaware History: Economic Development." Mimeographed, Newark, Del., 1939.

Renshaw, Patrick. *The Wobblies.* Garden City, N.Y.: Doubleday & Co., 1967.

Reps, John W. *The Making of Urban America.* Princeton, N.J.: Princeton University Press, 1965.

Richmond, Mary E. *Friendly Visiting Among the Poor.* New York: Macmillan & Co., 1899.

Rothman, David J. *Discovery of the Asylum: Social Order and Disorder in the New Republic.* Boston: Little, Brown & Co., 1971.

Scharf, J. Thomas. *History of Delaware, 1609–1888.* 2 vols. Philadelphia: L. J. Richards & Co., 1888.

Semi-Centennial Memoir of the Harlan & Hollingsworth Company, A. Wilmington, Del., 1886.

Shlakman, Vera. *Economic History of a Factory Town.* New York: Octagon, 1969.

Silliman, Charles A. *The Hospital.* Wilmington, Del., 1966.

Thernstrom, Stephen. *Poverty and Progress.* Cambridge, Mass.: Harvard University Press, 1964.

Tilly, Charles, et al. *Race and Residence in Wilmington, Delaware.* New York: Teachers College, Columbia University, 1965.

Tocqueville, Alexis de. *Democracy in America.* 2 vols. New York: Knopf, 1945.

Turner, Henry C. *A Modern Political Boss or Government by Proxy.* Wilmington, Del., 1896.

Tyler, David B. *The American Clyde.* Newark, Del.: University of Delaware Press, 1958.

United States Bureau of the Census. *Thirteenth Census of the United States . . . 1910,* vols. 1, 2, 4, 9. Washington, D.C., 1913, 1913, 1914, 1914.

————. *Fourteenth Census of the United States . . . 1920,* vols. 1, 2, 3, 4. Washington, D.C., 1921, 1922, 1922, 1923.

United States Census Office. *Eighth Census of the United States . . . 1860, Manufactures.* Washington, D.C., 1865.

————. *Ninth Census of the United States . . . 1870,* vols. 1, 3. Washington, D.C., 1872, 1872.

————. *Tenth Census of the United States . . . 1880,* vols. 1, 2, 18, 20. Washington, D.C., 1883, 1883, 1886, 1886.

———. *Eleventh Census of the United States . . . 1890*, vols. 1, 2, *Manufacturing* lowest

Industries, vols. 1, 2. Washington, D.C., 1895, 1897, 1895, 1895.

———. *Twelfth Census of the United States . . . 1900*, vols. 1, 2, 7, 8. Washington, D.C., 1901, 1902, 1902, 1902.

Ward, Christopher, *One Little Man*. New York: Harper & Bros., 1926.

Warner, Arthur E. *A Historical Sketch of Economic Developments in Wilmington, Delaware and Its Environs*. Newark, Del.: Wilmington Development Council, 1962.

Warner, Emalea P. *Childhood Memories*. Wilmington, Del., 1939.

Warner, Sam B. *The Private City: Philadelphia in Three Periods of Its Growth*. Philadelphia: University of Pennsylvania Press, 1968.

———. *Streetcar Suburbs: The Process of Growth in Boston, 1870–1900*. Cambridge, Mass.: Harvard University Press, 1962.

Welde, Charles H. *History of the Wilmington Fire Department*. Wilmington, Del.: Homer Barry Press, 1897.

Weslager, C. A. *Brandywine Springs, Rise and Fall of a Delaware Resort*. Wilmington, Del.: Hambleton Co., 1949.

———. *Delaware's Forgotten River: The Story of the Christina*. Wilmington, Del.: Hambleton Co., 1947.

———. *The Richardsons of Delaware*. Wilmington, Del.: Knebel Press, 1957.

Wiebe, Robert. *The Search for Order: 1877–1920*. New York: Hill & Wang, 1968.

Wilmington City Directory, 1814, 1845, 1853, 1857, 1868–69, 1880–81, 1883–84, 1885–1910.

Wolf, George A. *Industrial Wilmington*. Wilmington, Del., 1898.

Wrigley, Edmund. *The Workingman's Way to Wealth; A Practical Treatise on Building Associations*. Philadelphia: James K. Simon, 1869.

Index